HENRY...
SWEET HENRY

A MUSICAL COMEDY
IN TWO ACTS

Book by
NUNNALLY JOHNSON

Music and Lyrics by
BOB MERRILL

Based upon the Novel
"THE WORLD OF HENRY ORIENT"
by NORA JOHNSON

SAMUEL FRENCH, INC.
25 West 45th Street NEW YORK 10036
7623 Sunset Boulevard HOLLYWOOD 90046
LONDON *TORONTO*

MUSIC AND LYRICS BY BOB MERRILL

PRINTED IN U. S. A.

Press and bindery of The Conway Printing Co
New York

PREMIERE PERFORMANCE, OCTOBER 23, 1967

THE PALACE THEATRE

under the direction of

MESSRS. NEDERLANDER

EDWARD SPECTER PRODUCTIONS

and

NORMAN TWAIN

present

HENRY . . . SWEET HENRY

Book by NUNNALLY JOHNSON

Music and Lyrics by BOB MERRILL

Based upon the Novel

"THE WORLD OF HENRY ORIENT"

by NORA JOHNSON

Scenery and Lighting by ROBERT RANDOLPH

Costumes by ALVIN COLT

Musical Direction and Vocal Arrangements by SHEPARD COLEMAN
Orchestrations by EDDIE SAUTER

Dance Music by
WILLIAM GOLDENBERG *and* MARVIN HAMLISCH

Hair Styles Designed by ERNEST ADLER

Production Stage Manager—WILLIAM DODDS

Choreography by MICHAEL BENNETT

Entire Production Directed by GEORGE ROY HILL

CAST

(In Order of Appearance)

KAFRITZ . . . . *Alice Playten*
VALERIE BOYD . . . . *Robin Wilson*
MISS COONEY . . . . *Barbara Beck*
MARIAN GILBERT . . . . *Neva Small*
HENRY ORIENT . . . . *Don Ameche*
STELLA . . . . *Louise Lasser*
MRS. GILBERT . . . . *Trudy Wallace*
USHERETTE . . . . *Julie Sargant*
MRS. BOYD . . . . *Carol Bruce*
RUSS . . . . *John Mineo*
CAPTAIN KENNETH . . . . *George NeJame*
HAL . . . . *Robert Iscove*
POLICEMAN . . . . *Gerard Brentte*
MR. BOYD . . . . *Milo Boulton*
POLICEMAN . . . . *Charles Rule*
BIG VAL . . . . *K. C. Townsend*

The entire action takes place in present day New York City.

ACT ONE

Scene 1: A Street in New York City
"Academic Fugue" . . . . *Company*
Scene 2: Locker Room
"In Some Little World" . . . . *Val*
Scene 3: Central Park Zoo
"Pillar to Post" . . . . *Orient, Stella*
Scene 4: Two Bedrooms
"Here I Am" . . . . *Val*
Scene 5: Concert Hall
Scene 6: Val's Bedroom
"Whereas" . . . . *Val, Gil*
Scene 7: Telephone Booths
Scene 8: Luncheonette
"I Wonder How It Is To Dance
With a Boy" . . . . *Gil and Girls*
Scene 9: Street Telephone Booth
"Nobody Steps on Kafritz" . . . . *Kafritz*

Scene 10: Orient's Apartment—Exterior and Interior
"Henry Sweet Henry" .... *Val, Gil*
"Woman in Love" .... *Val, Gil*
"The People Watchers" .... *Company*

ACT TWO

Scene 1: Boyd's Living Room
Scene 2: Washington Square
"Weary Near to Dyin' " .... *Val and Hippies*
Scene 3: Orient's Apartment
Scene 4: Boyd's Living Room
Scene 5: Exterior School and Locker Room
"Poor Little Person" .... *Kafritz, Girls and Knickerbocker Greys*
"I'm Blue Too" .... *Val, Gil*
Scene 6: Cocktail Bar
"To Be Artistic" .... *Orient, Mrs. Boyd*
Scene 7: Exterior Orient's Apartment
Scene 8: Boyd's Living Room
Scene 9: Orient's Bedroom
"Forever" .... *Orient*
Scene 10: Val's Bedroom
"Do You Ever Go to Boston" .... *Val*
Finale: Knickerbocker Grey Happening
"Here I Am" (Reprise)

Henry . . . Sweet Henry

ACT ONE

Scene 1

On the first note of the overture, the House Curtain goes out, revealing the Show Curtain. Later, toward the end of the overture, the lights Upstage of the show scrim bleed through showing a New York street with the skyline at the rear of the stage. The Show Curtain goes out. Pia, *a young girl, enters up right carrying school books. She goes down right to wait for the school bus.*

Pia. (*Sings.*)
FACTUS, FACTUM, FACTU, FACTI
I DON'T SAY LATIN STINKS EXACTLY.
LATUS, LATI, LATUM, TOO
I THINK THAT I WILL LOSE A SCREW.

(*Other* Girls *enter and start to gather at the bus stop while* People *start to make their crosses as businessmen, lady calling for a taxi, nursemaid, grocery boys, etc.*)

Becky.
LA MIENNE, LA TIENNE, LA SIENNE, LA LEUR,
Joyce.
LA MERE, LE PERE, MADAM, MONSIEUR.
Lori.
WHEN I TRANSLATE FRENCH I THINK
Alice, Baayork, Chris.
LA BORE, LA NUTS, LA CRAP, LA STINK.

(*MUSIC interlude.*)

Priscilla. Taxi! Taxi!
Becky. Hi, Kafritz!
Kafritz. Hi!
Girls. (*Sing.*)
H_2O PLUS SO_2 MAKES H_2SO_3 FOR YOU,
AN UGLY MASS OF DEADLY GAS

WHICH I WILL TAKE IF I DON'T PASS.
I DON'T REALLY GIVE A DAMN
ABOUT A PARALLELOGRAM.
IF ANYONE HAS GOT A NOOSE
I'LL HANG BY MY HYPOTENUSE.

(VAL *enters Up Left carrying her books and papers in a paper shopping bag.*)

BECKY. Where's the bus?
KAFRITZ. Here comes Tubby!
LORI. What a mess!
GINA. Look at the coat!
JOY. She can't even keep her shoe on!
JOYCE. Slob!
TERRY. What's the answer to number four?
VAL. (*Going to the* GIRLS.) Is that your Latin homework? Can I copy it? (*She takes paper from* TERRY. *Squats on the floor.*) Anybody got a pencil?
JOY. Here.
VAL. Thanks. (*Takes pencil and starts to copy.*)
KAFRITZ. You can't hand that in, in pencil, stupid!
GIRLS. (*Sing.*)
FACTUS, FACTUM, FACTU, FACTI
I DON'T SAY LATIN STINKS EXACTLY.
LATUS, LATI, LATUM, TOO
I THINK THAT I WILL LOSE A SCREW.

(*The BUS enters Left and stops Center. All the* GIRLS *run and jump on the bus, except* VAL, *who is slow in gathering her books and papers together.*)

VAL. (*Looking for her shoe.*) Hey, where's my shoe? Anybody seen my shoe? (*Runs and gets on the bus. She goes up and down the aisle looking for her shoe.*)

(*MUSIC underscoring.*)

GIRLS. (*Sing as the BUS takes them to school.*)
FACTUS, FACTUM, FACTU, FACTI
I DON'T SAY LATIN STINKS EXACTLY

H_2O PLUS SO_3 MAKES H_2SO_3 FOR YOU
AN UGLY MASS OF DEADLY GAS
WHICH I WILL TAKE IF I DON'T PASS

<table>
<tr><td></td><td>I DON'T REALLY GIVE A DAMN</td></tr>
<tr><td>LATUS, LATI, LATUM TOO</td><td>ABOUT A PARALLELO-GRAM</td></tr>
<tr><td></td><td>IF ANYONE HAS GOT A NOOSE</td></tr>
<tr><td>I THINK THAT I WILL LOSE A SCREW.</td><td>I'LL HANG BY MY HY-POTENUSE.</td></tr>
</table>

(*The BUS stops and all the* GIRLS *jump off the bus except* VAL, *who is still looking for her shoe.* TERRY *ready to jump off.*)

VAL. Where's my shoe?
KAFRITZ. It's in the back!

(*The BUS drives off with* VAL *going to the rear of the bus for her shoe. The bus is replaced by LOCKERS, which come from Right and Left. In between them is a door, the entrance to the school, above which hangs an American flag.*)

GIRLS. (*As they come running through the door.*)
ICH BIN DU BIST
IHR SEID SIE IST
I MUST BE A MASOCHIST
MIT ICH NIN DU BIST
UN IHR SEID
I AHM COMMITTING ZOO-IZ-SEID.

LA MIENNE, LA TIENNE, LA SIENNE, LA LEUR
LA MERE, LE PERE, MADAM, MONSIEUR.
WHEN I TRANSLATE FRENCH I THINK
LA BORE, LA NUTS, LA CRAP, LA STINK.
I'LL DRINK SOME
INK AND DIE!

BLACKOUT

ACT ONE

SCENE 2

Locker room, Norton School. In the Center of the Stage is a door, with an American flag hanging above. To each side of the door are brightly colored lockers. Downstage of the lockers are two benches.

KAFRITZ. (*Downstage of the Left bench.*) Girls! Girls, I can get any girl who wants it a date for the Knickerbocker Greys' Annual Happening. There are still some very cute boys available. My service fee is a dollar fifteen.

(VAL *runs through the door, late again. As she gets inside the door, her paper bag breaks and notebooks, books, papers, composition books, comic books, etc. fall to the floor.*)

VAL. Any of you guys seen my shoe? (*No one answers. Goes Left to* KAFRITZ.) Kafritz, please give me my shoe.

KAFRITZ. (*Jumping down off the bench.*) How would you like to offer a reward?

VAL. (*Desperately.*) Please! I'll be late again.

MISS COONEY. (*Entering Right.*) First bell, girls.

KAFRITZ. Thank you, Miss Cooney. (*She exits Left.*)

VAL. Kafritz, you— (*She begins to take a swing at* KAFRITZ *with her racket.*)

MISS COONEY. Valerie, what is it now?

VAL. (*Hopping Center.*) Somebody pinched my shoe in the bus.

MISS COONEY. What was it last time, your belt?

VAL. (*Starts to pick up papers from the floor.*) Well, can I help it if this school is full of burglars?

MISS COONEY. You'll do anything for an effect, (*Goes Left, Downstage of* VAL.) anything to draw attention to yourself.

VAL. They pinch my shoes, they pinch my belt, they grab my books, they make me late for class, what can I do?

MISS COONEY. Sometimes I wonder why on earth Norton ever accepted you.

VAL. Then throw me out, shoot me, I don't care any more. It's a rotten world, anyway.

MISS COONEY. That's impertinent, Valerie. Clean that up and report to Miss Beardsley's office after class.

(MISS COONEY *exits. A group of* GIRLS, *Right, giggle and go to classes.* GILBERT *comes forward.*)

GILBERT. I think I know where it is. (*She goes to the Right lockers and gets Val's shoe from the top. She takes it to* VAL.)

VAL. Thanks.

GILBERT. That's all right. You're new this year, aren't you?

VAL. I'm always new. This is my seventh school.

GILBERT. Your seventh?

VAL. I can't integrate, they say—even with white children. Say, what was that "Happening" Kafritz was talking about?

GILBERT. That's what they call the annual dance with the Knickerbocker Greys. (VAL *makes a retching noise.* GILBERT *crosses to* VAL *and kneels Right of her.*) That's what I say!

VAL. Have you ever danced?

GILBERT. Not with a boy.

VAL. Me neither. You know what I saw some of those boys doing at the bus stop the other day? They were having a burping contest!

GILBERT. They are really so disgusting.

VAL. (*Rises, hand full of papers.*) Do you know Paul Henreid?

GILBERT. Is he in the Knickerbocker Greys?

VAL. (*Goes Left to her locker.*) No, he's on some of the olden times movies on the late show. (*She opens the door and reveals the junkiest locker in the school. Puts papers on bench. She takes off her coat and piles it on top of everything else.*)

GILBERT. Oh, I remember now. He's wonderful. The world was really different in the olden days, don't you think?

VAL. (*Returns Center to* GILBERT.) He was really cool on the late late the other night. When he'd light a cigarette, he'd light two, one for Bette Davis so she wouldn't have to light it herself.

GILBERT. I wouldn't mind going to the dance with somebody like that.

VAL. Or with Charles Boyer, or Herbert Marshall or George Brent.

GILBERT. How do you get to see all those shows?

VAL. My parents aren't there and I watch them all night.

GILBERT. Are they divorced?

VAL. No, are yours?

GILBERT. (*Nods.*) Oh, a long time ago. I live with my mother.

VAL. My dad's in some kind of international business so they're away most of the time.

GILBERT. Where is your home?

VAL. We live in hotels mostly. I stay at the Carlyle while my parents are gone. You see, Dad has to travel a lot and Mom's crazy about him, so she goes with him everywhere. But do you know she writes me a letter every day?

GILBERT. Honest?

VAL. No matter where she is. Sometimes six and seven pages, all about what they're doing and everything. She's one of the ten best dressed women in the world, you know.

GILBERT. No kidding?

VAL. And if she makes it one more time, they're going to put her in the Hall of Fame.

(*The second BELL rings and* GILBERT *leaps up, runs to put some papers in Val's locker. Then she runs and gets her books from the Right bench.*)

GILBERT. Oh, golly, there's the second bell. Aren't you coming?

VAL. I've got study first period.

GILBERT. Okay. (*She almost leaves, but turns back to* VAL.) I'm Marian Gilbert.

VAL. I'm Valerie Boyd.

GILBERT. I'm very pleased to meet you.

VAL. I'm glad to meet you too.

GILBERT. Bye now.

VAL. Hey, how about meeting me Saturday in Central Park and go adventuring?

GILBERT. Adventuring?

VAL. Sure, there's a whole other world out there on Saturdays. It's lots of fun.

GILBERT. I don't know if I can. I'll have to ask my mother.

VAL. (*Disappointed.*) Okay.

GILBERT. Bye. (*She exits Right.*)

VAL. Bye. (*MUSIC begins.* VAL *picks up more papers, books, etc., and takes them to the locker. MUSIC underscoring. Some of the papers fall out of the locker. Looking down at the mess on the floor, she sings:*)

IN SOME LITTLE WORLD
STUFF STAYS UP
IN SOME LITTLE WORLD
AND EV'RYTHING'S IN PLACE
IT SHOWS ON EV'RY FACE
THAT IT'S A NICE LITTLE WORLD.
STUFF'LL STAY ON A SHELF
PRACTIC'LY BY ITSELF.
GIVE IT A TRY.
DO YOU KNOW WHY?
WELL IT'S 'CAUSE
NOBODY ROCKS YOUR BOAT—THAT'S WHY!

IN SOME LITTLE WORLD
THINGS STAY PUT,
IN SOME LITTLE WORLD
THERE'S SOMETHIN' IN THE AIR
THAT MAKES A PERSON CARE
FOR MORE THAN THEIR LITTLE WORLD.
MY STUFF GETS WRECKED
AND I SUSPECT
IT ISN'T ONLY ACCIDENTALLY.
IT'S THIS LITTLE WORLD
I KEEP ON FIGHT'N
GOTTA FIND A WORLD
THAT I FEEL RIGHT IN
THAT'S A LITTLE WORLD
THE ONLY LITTLE WORLD FOR ME.

MISS COONEY. (*Entering Left.*) Valerie, I told you to clean that up!

VAL. I did, but it fell out again.

MISS COONEY. You don't make things any better by lying, Valerie!

(*She exits Right.* VAL *cleans everything up and closes her locker door.*)

VAL.
IN SOME LITTLE WORLD
NO MISS COONEY HOUNDS YOU TO DEATH.
MISS COONEYS GET THROWN IN
A COONEY LOONEY BIN
'CAUSE THEY JUST RUIN THIS WORLD
AND WHEN A KID COMES TO SCHOOL
MINUS HER HOMEWORK
THEY GIVE HER A BREAK.
HOW MUCH DOES THAT TAKE?
I KNOW THE LAST THING THEY'D DO
IS PINCH HER SHOE.

IN SOME LITTLE WORLD
CHARLES BOYER APPEARS IN THE DAWN
TO TELL ME HE IS FREE
AT LAST TO MARRY ME.
OH BOY, THAT'S SOME LITTLE WORLD.
WE WALK THROUGH WIND,
WE WALK THROUGH RAIN,
WE BRUSH AWAY OUR TEARS AND KISS.
DOESN'T THAT LITTLE WORLD
SOUND REALLY NIFTY,
EVEN IF IT'S ONLY FIFTY FIFTY?
ANY LITTLE WORLD
HAS GOT TO BE BETTER THAN THIS.
(*She exits Left.*)

ACT ONE

SCENE 3

At the end of the song, VAL *runs out Left, and the LOCKERS move out. In a SPOT behind the locker on Stage Left is revealed* HENRY ORIENT, *a mysterious figure in a slouch hat and nineteen thirties trench coat, wearing dark glasses. He stands absolutely still, like a movie poster. As the audience catches sight of him, the full orchestra swells into the strains of FOREVER. He holds for a moment, and then the mood is broken as the theme lightens and the ZOO SET falls into place, and* PEOPLE *start walking through the park, on bicycles, carrying sailboats, etc. A bench is Center Stage.* HENRY *casually removes a pack of cigarettes from his pocket as* VAL, *from Left, starts across, tapping her way with a cane and a tin cup. She is a sight to wring the hardest of hearts, a beautiful child in a ratty mink coat. Her eyes are out of focus and on her face is the sad, sweet smile of a saint.*

VAL. Alms! Alms! For the love of Allah, Alms! (*A* WOMAN *gives her a coin. MUSIC out.*) God bless you and keep you forever, kind sir . . . Alms! Alms!

(*She taps her way Right, looks at* HENRY, *who ignores her. At the same time* GIL *enters Up Left, also tapping her way with a cane and a tin cup.*)

GILBERT. Unclean! Unclean! I've got leprosy of the eyes! Unclean!

(HENRY *is taking two cigarettes from his pack and is lighting the two of them together as* GIL *passes him.* GIL *looks. MUSIC under. She gets just beyond him, realizes what she has seen and turns, forgetting her blindness for a moment to gawk. The music swells into the full strains of FOREVER.* HENRY *finishes lighting the cigarettes, notices* GIRLS *staring at him. The* GIRLS *run off Right.* HENRY *then turns to hand his second cigarette to someone else, except that there is no one else. Holding the two cigarettes, he lifts his dark glasses and peers about him.*)

ORIENT. Darling? Darling?

(*MUSIC out.*)

STELLA. (*Off.*) Henry?

ORIENT. (*He sees her out of sight in the lion house. Goes Right toward the door.*) What the hell are you doing in there—carissima?

STELLA. (*Points Off Left.*) I thought I saw George.

ORIENT. (*Goes* C. *He looks around nervously. Puts on his dark glasses again.*) I thought you said he was playing golf.

STELLA. He is, (*She enters slowly.*) but sometimes he picks up. Do you really think we're safe here, darling?

ORIENT. I can't guarantee it, no, (*Few steps Right to her.*) but sure—we'd be a lot less likely to run into your husband in my apartment.

STELLA. No, darling, I couldn't. I really couldn't. (*She moves Downstage, peering about like a frightened bird. He goes to* STELLA.)

ORIENT. (*Takes off glasses.*) Sweetheart, don't you want me to set your beautiful poem to music?

STELLA. You know I do, darling! It's the dream of my life!

ORIENT. Then will you kindly remember that a composer has to sit at a piano to compose?

STELLA. Not today, darling, please!

ORIENT. He can't do it surrounded by lions and tigers.

STELLA. I know, I know . . .

ORIENT. I mean even the fellow who wrote "Only God Can Make a Tree" didn't COMPOSE it in a tree! (*Goes Left to the bench, Upstage of* STELLA.) He had to go back to the piano. In his apartment. (*Sits.*)

STELLA. (*Crosses to bench, sits.*) But GOING there, Henry!—in the STREET—crossing the SIDEWALK—suppose somebody from Scarsdale saw me!

ORIENT. (*Bitterly.*) You mean we're going to spend all our time meeting in zoos and laundromats? (*Sings.*)

WE'VE BEEN FLEEING FROM PILLAR TO POST
BEING CHASED THROUGH NEW YORK BY SOME
GHOST
IF NOT SOAKED TO THE SKIN
WE HAVE SURELY BEEN IN DRAFTS A LOT.

WE HAVE KISSED WITH BOTH PASSION AND FRENZY
ON THE RAMPS OF GRAND CENTRAL AND PENNSY
UNDER ROCKS, UNDER TREES
AND HAD INTIMACIES IN SCHRAFFTS A LOT.

IN THE MUSIC HALL'S VERY LAST ROWS
WE HAVE PUT ON SOME INTERESTING SHOWS.
WE HAVE OFTEN BEEN CAUSE FOR
WILD APPLAUSE AND LAFFS A LOT.

THRU THE PARK, IN A HANSOM AGAINST
THE WIND WE'VE SPED.
WE HAVE CERTAINLY CIRCLED THAT COURSE A
LOT.
PEOPLE TELL ME I SMELL LIKE A HORSE A LOT.
(*Rises.*)
IT'S BEEN PILLAR TO POST
BUT NEVER TO BED!

(*Speaks.*)
Darling, recite your poem for me.

STELLA. Now?

ORIENT. Now.

STELLA. (*Recites.*)

My heart boom booms
With a crashing din
When flesh meets flesh
And skin meets skin.

ORIENT. (*Long pause.*) Magnificent! Let's go to my apartment.

STELLA. (*Rises.*) Oh, *no* darling, I can't.

ORIENT. (*Crosses Right few steps.*) Here we go again . . . meeting in funeral parlors . . . Gristedes' . . . (STELLA *sits as he sings.*)

IN THE BACK OF SAINT PAT'S AND SAINT LUKE'S
ALL THOSE LOOKS OF DISDAIN AND REBUKES
(*Sits.*)
AS IF YOU WERE SOME TART AND I WAS
JACK THE RIPPER.
AND AT TEMPLE EMANU-EL
I AM CERTAIN THAT RABBI COULD TELL
HE WAS STUCK WITH A COUPLE OF GENTILES
FOR YOM KIPPUR.
(*Rises.*)

FOR A MODERN DON JUAN AND
SIR LAUNCELOT
I DON'T SEEM TO GET OUT OF MY
PANTS A LOT.

IT'S FROM PILLAR TO POST
BUT NEVER TO BED!
IT'S FROM PILLAR TO POST
BUT NEVER TO BED!

(*He goes to the bench and puts his dark glasses down, sits.*) Now look, darling, it's Saturday—not a soul in town. Now you can lie down on the floor of the taxi and I'll get out first and take a look around— (*She moans.*) Sweetheart, now it's only thirteen feet from the curb to the door—I measured it this morning—and if you hike up your dress a bit and make a smart dash—

STELLA. (*Surrender.*) Henry, will you be gentle with me?

ORIENT. Oh, you brave little girl!

(VAL *enters from the lion house, Right. He rises, pulls* STELLA *up and they embrace.*)

VAL. (*Goes to Center, stops, looks at them in embrace.*) Is there anyone here within the sound of my voice?

(*So far as* ORIENT *is concerned, it's to hell with her, but* STELLA *is deeply touched.*)

STELLA. Henry . . .

ORIENT. (*Reluctantly, crosses Right to* VAL.) Can I help you?

VAL. If you would be so kind, sir. There was once a bench around here where I spent many beautiful sunny hours before my tragedy.

ORIENT. (*Leading her Left to bench.*) Is that it?

VAL. (*Sits.*) Ah, yes, this is it—my old good friend! How I've missed you! Were you sitting on it, sir?

ORIENT. (*Crossing back to* STELLA.) It's all right, we were just leaving—

VAL. (*Rising.*) Oh, please! I didn't mean to disturb you. Do sit again, won't you? (STELLA *motions to him; resentfully he sits with her on the bench again.*)

STELLA. Thank you, dear.

VAL. (*A benediction, goes Upstage to bench.*) And may you sit on and on together—side by side—forever—and may God give you both the happiness that was mine before that fatal day when our bus went over the cliff. (*On that cheery note, she goes Up Center.*)

STELLA. Did you ever see anything so sad!

ORIENT. Very rough! (BOTH *start to rise.*) Come on, let's get the hell out—

VAL. (*Returning, Down Center.*) But I was the lucky one. (ORIENT *and* STELLA *sit again.*) The others are all dead—burned to a crisp in the flames that enveloped it like some avenging fiend. But I escaped—flung, through God's mercy, a hundred feet through the air and into a haystack—

STELLA. Oh, my God!

VAL. (*Starts Right, but stops.*) In which there was a pitchfork—

STELLA. Oh, no!

VAL. (*Starts Right, stops again.*) It penetrated my spinal column. (*She taps her way into the lion house.*)

STELLA. (*Holding the base of her spinal column.*) Oh! Oh!

ORIENT. (*Desperately.*) Will you come on!

(BOTH *rise.*)

STELLA. Oh, Henry!

(*This time* GILBERT *emerges from the lion house and stops with a look of exaltation on her face.*)

GILBERT. Hark! Hark!

ORIENT. Hark? Hark?

GILBERT. Was that not a lark?

ORIENT. What the hell is this? A picnic?

GILBERT. How well I remember how they used to nestle in our weeping willow. (*She wanders off Left.*)

STELLA. Those poor children—

(VAL *enters from the lion's house.*)

ORIENT. Look, if we were in my bedroom we wouldn't be able to see 'em.

VAL. (*Going Left.*) Oh willow, willow, weep for me!

STELLA. Oh, I do!

VAL. Weep only for me! (*Exits Left.*)

ORIENT. (*To* STELLA.) Are you coming or not?

GILBERT. (*Entering Left, goes Right.*) Heathcliff! (*Exits Upstage of lion's house.*)

STELLA. Don't you see how impossible it is now, darling? Maybe I could see you next Friday night, darling, after your concert.

ORIENT. But sweetheart—

STELLA. George is going to be out of town in a golf tournament and I promise you, I'll come straight to Carnegie Hall. Oh, darling. (*They embrace.*) I've got to get out of here. (STELLA *starts to run off Right.*)

ORIENT. But what am I going to do this afternoon?

STELLA. (*Turns back to him.*) And remember—don't call after six!

(*MUSIC underscoring.*)

ORIENT. But, darling. . . . (*Runs after her.*) Darling! (*He gives up. His shoulders slump dejectedly as* VAL *and* GILBERT *appear, wide-eyed and sympathetic.* HENRY *comes back slowly to the bench, where he has left his dark glasses.* VAL *picks them up and hands them to him.*) Thank you! (*He starts off Right, only to stop a moment later; turns and slowly, ominously staring at the two* GIRLS, *it having dawned on him finally that his glasses were handed to him by a blind child. Under his gaze, the* GIRLS *look at each other, realize the game is up and dash off.* HENRY, *furious, shouts after them.*) You little punks!

BLACKOUT

ACT ONE

SCENE 4

Two bedrooms. The GIRLS *run Downstage with telephones,* GILBERT *from Up Right and* VAL *from Up Left. They begin talking at once.* GILBERT'S *bed comes in from the Right, Upstage of* GILBERT. *A messy bed, with a night table and a lamp to its Right, comes in from the Left above* VAL. *The wall of Val's room is decorated with her olden time film idols. Gilbert's wall is covered with pennants, clippings, pictures, scraps of this and that, etc.*

GILBERT. I nearly died when he lighted those two cigarettes.
VAL. And did you notice those eyes, the way they seemed to look right through you?
GILBERT. X-ray eyes, they call 'em. Robert Taylor had them on Greta Garbo the other evening.
VAL. You know what I think?

(*Both* GIRLS *go Upstage.* VAL *sits in the middle of her bed, cross-legged.* GILBERT *kneels on her bed.*)

GILBERT. What?
VAL. I think that was really a romantic tragedy situation.
GILBERT. That's exactly what I think. They were childhood sweethearts and he went to war and she married someone else she really didn't love.
VAL. A lifelong invalid who couldn't get along without her.
GILBERT. Or an Orthodox Catholic who won't give her a divorce.
VAL. That was probably their final parting this afternoon.
GILBERT. Did you get your letter today?
VAL. What letter?
GILBERT. From your mother.
VAL. Oh, sure, every single day. Wait a minute. (*Puts phone down on night table. Picks up a magazine from the bottom shelf of the table.*) This is a real fat one. Wait till I open it. (*Tears the magazine near the phone.*) Want to hear some of it?
GILBERT. Sure.
VAL. It starts out: "Hello, Pretty Thing"—that's what they call me—really—Pretty Thing.
GILBERT. I think that's sweet.
VAL. She's in Greece now and they really miss me.
GILBERT. She sounds awfully nice.
VAL. She really is. Wait till you meet her.
GILBERT. Oh, Mom says you can come to dinner Friday and she'll take us to a concert or something, okay?

VAL. Okay. Gee, can you imagine how lonely he must be now?

GILBERT. Who?

VAL. The man in the park.

GILBERT. Oh, yeah.

VAL. (*Rises. Breaks Downstage.*) I wish I knew him better so I could write him a letter.

GILBERT. You really would?

VAL. I wouldn't have to tell him how old I was. I'd just let him know how I understood and all.

GILBERT. That would be a very nice thing to do, Val.

VAL. I mean maybe if he just knew I was here and really cared, it might comfort him.

GILBERT. I'm sure it would.

MRS. GILBERT. (*Calling from Off Right.*) Marian . . . dinner's ready!

GILBERT. I gotta go now. I'll call you later, okay?

VAL. Okay.

GILBERT. Bye.

VAL. Bye. (*Hangs up. MUSIC underscoring.* GILBERT *has run Off Right; the lights have dimmed on her room.* VAL *puts her phone on her night table. Looks front and sings.*)

HERE I AM
HEY SOMEBODY
HERE I AM, HERE I AM!

I DON'T KNOW YOU
YOU DON'T KNOW ME
BUT HERE I AM.
SOMEBODY SOMEWHERE, HURRY,
FIND ME.
SOMEBODY SOMEWHERE
LOVE ME BLINDLY.

THERE YOU ARE
THOUGH I DON'T KNOW WHERE YOU ARE
THERE YOU ARE
WONDERING WILL
SHE EVER APPEAR,
BUT HERE I AM.

HEY SOMEBODY
WHO I DON'T EVEN KNOW.
HEY SOMEBODY
THOUGH YOU MUST NEED ME SO
PLEASE TRY NOT TO CRY SOMEBODY
MY SOMEBODY

HI SOMEBODY
HERE I AM.

WHEREVER YOU ARE
AT THE MOMENT
I SEND YOU SOME KISSES AND LOVE.

PLEASE TRY NOT TO CRY SOMEBODY
MY SOMEBODY
HI SOMEBODY
HERE I AM.

(*TRUMPETS.*)

BLACKOUT

ACT ONE

SCENE 5

Carnegie Hall. Up Right there are two stairs on which a singing CHORUS *is standing. The men are in evening jackets; the ladies, in long black gowns. In front of the group are microphones and white stands with music. Stage Left, we see four masseur tables. Next to each table is a microphone and a white music stand with music. In front of each table stands a* MAN *dressed in a black choir robe. Upstage of the tables are* MEN *in evening jackets and* LADIES *in black gowns. At the rear of the Stage is a huge picture of Henry Orient. He enters Right, goes Center and bows to the audience.*

ORIENT. Mesdames, Messieurs. Welcome to the new new music. (STELLA, *sitting in the Stage Right box, applauds.*) The music of natural sounds ripped from the very gut of life—the music of the street, the factory, the home—the whispery hum of the vacuum cleaner, the tinkle of a child in the bathroom, the melancholy belch of a lonely drunk in the wrong room— All homely sounds indeed, but of the very weft and woft of life. And if there should be any here who lack the courage to face this crash-through into true musical freedom, may I humbly suggest that you leave now, for your place is not here, but in Lincoln Center, or some other such municipal soup-kitchen of mass culture. Tonight, for those whose eyes are on the distant horizon, I beg to offer my new opus, a symphonic history of homo sapiens from his emergence from the primeval slime to five-thirty this afternoon, as scored for and played upon the human body. The first movement—Cosmic Silence.

(MUSICIANS *Upstage of the masseur tables move to the* MEN *Downstage of the tables and remove their choir robes. Now the* MEN *are dressed in white shorts, white false cuffs, white collars and black shoes and socks. The* MEN *lie down on the masseur tables as the* MUSICIANS *take their place Upstage of them.* ORIENT *turns Upstage, picks up his baton and taps the music stand. He then begins to conduct. After several measures, all* MUSICIANS *turn a page. At the same moment, an* USHER, *with a flashlight, shows* VAL, GILBERT *and* MRS. GILBERT *to three seats in the lower box.*)

VAL. Are we late?
GILBERT. Doesn't look to me as if we're late.
VAL. (*To the* USHER.) Hey, has it started yet?
USHER. Shhhh! Please!
GILBERT. Mom, why don't you go in first?
VAL. I'll sit in the middle.
GILBERT. No, let me sit in the middle and Mom can look at my program.
VAL. But she can look at mine, I don't mind.
GILBERT. All right . . . don't make such a big deal.
USHER. Will you please sit down and try to be quiet?
GILBERT. Oh, I'm sorry. I didn't know it had started.

(*The* USHER *leaves.* ORIENT *has endured this ordeal with notable patience.*)

ORIENT. May we start again!

(*The* MUSICIANS *turn their pages back to the beginning and once more he begins to conduct.*)

GILBERT. Valerie Boyd, you've shaved your legs!
MRS. GILBERT. Marian, will you please be quiet!
GILBERT. You're going to get bristles.
VAL. Not if I keep shaving them.
GILBERT. But you're not so hairy. You're not half as hairy as Kafritz. Kafritz is the—
ORIENT. (*Turning to the* GIRLS.) If you don't keep quiet—
GIRLS. Eeeeeeeek!

(*They* ALL *recognize each other at the same time.*)

VAL. It's him!
ORIENT. Oh, no!
GILBERT. The man in the park—
VAL. With the lady.

STELLA. Oh, my God. (*She leaves the box.*)

VAL. There she is!

GILBERT. Miss—Miss—come back! Come back! (ORIENT, *helpless, watches* STELLA *leave.*) Oh, that's too bad!

ORIENT. (*After gaining his composure.*) The second movement—Man Emerges from the Muck.

BLACKOUT

ACTION FOR ORIENT'S "NEW MUSIC"

ALL.
BLIP-BLOOP-BLURP-GURGLE

ALL.
WIND-SSSHOOOOOOOOOOOSH

ALL.
BLIP-BLURPS-BLOOPS-GURGLES

ALL.
RAIN-BLOOP, BLOOPS

ALL.
DRIBBLES (BABIES)

ALL.
TEETH CLICKS

ALL.
PUT-PUT

BODY BEATERS.
BODY SLAPS

ALL.
KISS, KISS, KISS, KISS

BODIES.
UH

ALL.
CLUCK, CLUCK, CLUCK, CLUCK

BODIES.
UH

ALL.
CLUCK, CLUCK, CLUCK, CLUCK

BODIES.
UH, UH, UH, UH

ACT ONE

Scene 6

Val's bedroom in the Carlyle Hotel. As the LIGHTS come up, we see Val *passed out on the bed, Left. To the Left of the bed on a night table is a phonograph. A Henry Orient record album is on the bed. A matching night table, Right of the bed, holds a lamp and telephone. Up Center is an armoire. A vanity and chair are Right. The room is far from neat. On the back wall are huge photographs of Val's late late movie idols. A large three-sheet of Henry Orient's Carnegie Hall concert has been added.* Gilbert *is heard calling from Off Right.*

Gilbert. (*Off.*) Val? Val? (*She comes into the room and goes Left to the bed.*) Val! What's the matter?

Val. (*She points to the Orient poster.*) I'm in love.

Gilbert. (*Looks at the new poster.*) With that creep?

Val. (*Sits up.*) What do you mean, creep?

Gilbert. I thought you said his music was terrible.

Val. Oh, Gil, have you no soul? Of course it's terrible, but this is love! (*She clutches Henry's album to her breast.*) Oh, my beautiful adorable oriental Henry— (*Kisses album.*) Oh, moon of my delight! Isn't he divine?

Gilbert. You mean it's real love?

Val. Can't think of what else it could be. I can't sleep, I can't eat, I can't think of anything else.

Gilbert. If it's real love, then it's the most important thing in the whole world, isn't it?

Val. Of course.

Gilbert. It's got to be a secret then, hasn't it?

Val. Oh, it's got to be.

Gilbert. (*Going to vanity and looking in the drawers.*) Then we've got to make a blood pact never to betray our secret to anyone—all right?

Val. Okay. (*Rises.*) And we'll have a secret language. (*Takes bedspread off bed.*) His language—the mysterious language of the Orient!

(*Spreads the bedspread on the floor, Center.* Gilbert *had found a compass and brings it to* Val.)

Gilbert. Ah, so. . . . Ming-ching-ting-ching-ching-ting.

Val. Ming-ching-ting-ching-ching. . . . (*Looks at the sharp end of the compass.*) Do we have to really cut?

Gilbert. Of course. How can you have a sacred blood pact

without blood? (*Sticks her finger with the point of the compass.*) Wow! watch it! Not too hard; it hurts. (*Gives compass to* VAL.)

VAL. (*Punches her finger as* GILBERT *did.*) Pain! Pain! Pain!

GILBERT. And now, O Princess Cherry Blossom, the sacred oath.

(*They hold their fingers together. MUSIC.*)

VAL. I do solemnly swear that—what?

GILBERT. (*In absolute earnest.*) That whereas love is the most important thing in the whole wide world, especially true love—therefore, be it resolved that Valerie Campbell Boyd and Marian Byrnes Gilbert will lead a secret life in the name of one Henry Orient, the truly beloved of Miss Boyd.

VAL. I do.

GILBERT. And from the moment on, except during school and homework, we'll follow him everywhere he goes.

VAL. And study his whole life, both public and private—where he lives, who he sees—

GILBERT. And what he really thinks about when he's not practicing his art.

VAL. So help me God!

(*MUSIC out.* MRS. BOYD *is heard Off Right.*)

MRS. BOYD. Anybody home? (*Enters.*) Anybody home?

VAL. It's Mom!

(*Runs to her and into her arms, almost knocking her over.* GILBERT, *subdued by this fashionable jet-setter, picks up the bedspread and takes it back to the bed. Puts compass on night table.*)

MRS. BOYD. Careful, dear. Givenchy didn't design this dress for wrestling.

VAL. Why didn't you let me know?

MRS. BOYD. I'm sorry, darling, but you know how I hate writing letters. (VAL *quickly turns to see if* GILBERT *has heard her mother.* GILBERT *is trying to put the bedspread back on the bed.* MRS. BOYD *notices her.*) And who is that?

VAL. (*Goes Left and pulls* GILBERT *over the bed to her side.*) This is Marian Gilbert. She's my best friend.

MRS. BOYD. How are you, Marian?

GILBERT. Very well, thank you.

VAL. (*Rushing to her* MOTHER.) Where's Father?

MRS. BOYD. At the office, where else? Straight from the plane! But he's going to join us for dinner tonight. (*Turns* VAL *around.*)

A little surprise party, just for you! Dirty face! How would you like the Four Seasons?

VAL. Wow! (*Returns to* GILBERT'S *side.*) Can Gil go with us?

GILBERT. (*Quickly.*) Oh, thank you very much, but I have a previous engagement.

MRS. BOYD. (*Just as quickly.*) That's too bad, but we'll make it another time. (*Goes to vanity for her coat, purse and gloves.*) Now if you'll try to make yourself a little more presentable, we can run down to Bergdorf's now and pick up something for you tonight. (*To* GILBERT.) Goodbye, dear. I'm sure that we'll meet again. (*Exits Right.*)

VAL. Isn't she neat? (*Goes to armoire. Opens it.*) That's always the way it is when they get back— Four Seasons, Twenty-one— and just wait till you see the loot! Bergdorf's, Saks, Lord and Taylor—just about anything I want!

GILBERT. But what about—Henry?

VAL. We can do that some other time, can't we?

GILBERT. I guess so.

(MRS. BOYD *re-enters Right.*)

VAL. What about tomorrow?

GILBERT. (*Runs off Right, almost knocking down* MRS. BOYD.) Doesn't matter—

VAL. (*Calling off after her.*) Gil—Gil—

MRS. BOYD. Oops! Goodbye—er— (*To* VAL.) Is anything wrong?

VAL. Oh, no.

MRS. BOYD. I mean we don't want anything spoiling our party tonight, do we?

VAL. No, everything's wonderful really.

(*The TELEPHONE rings.*)

MRS. BOYD. Be a lamb and do hurry, darling. (*Picks up phone on the Right night table.*) Hello? Oh, darling! Where in God's name have you been? No, we were in Greece and it was deadly beyond words. (VAL *crosses Down Center.*) Even New York is better than Greece . . . (VAL *crosses to armoire.*) Tonight? Oh, no, not tonight, I'm afraid. The Boyds are having a little party of their own tonight. (*She blows a kiss to* VAL, *who is picking out shoes and a dress at the armoire.*) Oh, really? I had no idea they were in the States. (VAL *takes a dress to the bed.*) I hear he's really something special. Mm? Mm? You're really making it sound like the party of the year. Look, dear, may I call you back? I won't be five minutes. (*She hangs up and smiles at* VAL. VAL *smiles at her.*) What a bore!

VAL. That's all right.

MRS. BOYD. You know what your father always says! More deals are made at dinner parties than in the office—and I know he'll insist on going to this one. But if you want me to speak to him—

VAL. It's really all right, Mom.

MRS. BOYD. You really don't mind?

VAL. Aw, no—

MRS. BOYD. You are a darling, and now I've got to get started. (*She blows* VAL *a kiss and starts out, calling.*) Alice, would you plug in the steam iron and get the black silk dress out of the green bag?

(*She goes off.* VAL *sits on the bed alone, dejected. She picks up Orient's album as:*)

BLACKOUT

ACT ONE

SCENE 7

A telephone BOOTH in the Scarsdale depot lights up Stage Right. STELLA, *in a Mata Hari cloak and heavily veiled, enters it and dials. Another BOOTH comes on Downstage Left.* ORIENT *enters Left just in time to answer. He grabs the phone.*

ORIENT. Yes?

STELLA. (*Nervously.*) Henry?

ORIENT. No names, please. (STELLA *pulls veil down.*) Where are you?

STELLA. I'm in the station in Scarsdale. I'm catching the 11:20. George is playing golf.

ORIENT. Okay now, I've got it all worked out how we're going to tear off that little old song today without your being seen. (*She moans.*) Will you listen first, sweet, before you start whimpering?

STELLA. (*Tremulously.*) I'm sorry.

ORIENT. Now, when you get to Grand Central, take a taxi to Flynn's Fish Haven on the east side of Lexington between 62nd and 63rd. That's right around the corner from my place in the same block. Flynn's an old friend of mine— I throw him all my fish business—and he'll be looking for you.

STELLA. But he'll see me, darling—

ORIENT. Of course he'll see you, sweet—

STELLA. He might tell somebody—

ORIENT. Who the hell could he tell, sweetheart? He doesn't know anybody but other fish people. Anyway you only go through there to get down a ladder into the coal cellar.

STELLA. (*Startled.*) What coal-cellar?

ORIENT. Flynn's.

STELLA. Oh, no, darling, not in a coal-cellar—

ORIENT. Now, you don't have to worry about that, sweet. It's not even used for coal any more—just fish— But you have to go through it to get to the boiler-room, don't you see?

STELLA. Look, darling, have you ever thought of Newark—

ORIENT. Not while I'm in my right mind, sweet. I wouldn't cross the STATE LINE for—Sophia Loren.

STELLA. Oh, but not in a boiler-room, Henry.

ORIENT. If you'd be good enough to stop interrupting, sweetheart, it never even occurred to me to compose in the boiler-room. But that's how you have to get to the alley—

STELLA. Maybe we ought to make it another day, darling.

ORIENT. Listen, sweetheart— (*A pause to gain control.*) Do you want that goddamn poem set to music or not?

STELLA. I was only wondering if we'll have enough time.

ORIENT. We will if you don't yak it all away.

STELLA. But what if he picks up?

ORIENT. Listen, baby, either we take a hack at it today or I'm picking up! So make up your mind, kid, yes or no, and that'll be it, period.

STELLA. (*Crying.*) Go on.

ORIENT. You are my brave little love jug. Now where were we?

STELLA. In the—alley.

ORIENT. We're nearly home now, honey-bun. Once you're over that little barbed-wire fence that some nut stuck up there— (*A groan from* STELLA.) Then you're directly under my fire-escape! I'm afraid you'll have to take a little running jump for that drop ladder.

STELLA. (*Snapping.*) I can't do it, Henry! I can't do all that.

ORIENT. But I've got it all worked out for you, sweetheart.

STELLA. I'm sorry, but I'd better stay in Scarsdale.

ORIENT. (*In alarm.*) Hold it, now! Don't hang up, sweet! Don't you want to hear the rest of my plan?

STELLA. I'd be too scared.

ORIENT. (*Softly.*) You mean even with me at your side you'd be scared?

STELLA. But, Henry—you didn't say—

ORIENT. You and I, darling, are going together, side by side, down the ladder, through that alley, and up that fire-escape— (*Softly.*) to Paradise, macushla!

STELLA. Oh, darling!

ORIENT. Now off you go, my little bundle of goodies, and I'll meet you in the fish house.

STELLA. You won't be long, will you?

ORIENT. I'll be right on your tail, sweet.

BLACKOUT

ACT ONE

SCENE 8

Luncheonette. The entrance is Up Left Center. To the Left is a soda fountain with three high stools. Just Right of the door and Downstage of a large store window is a table with two chairs. Another table, with two chairs, is Down Right. GIRLS *are seated at the fountain and at the tables.* GILBERT *enters and goes to the table Down Right.*

GILBERT. (*Sings.*)

I WONDER HOW IT IS TO DANCE WITH A BOY,
A DREAM I KEEP SEEIN'
IS ME 'N A BOY.
I WONDER HOW IT IS TO DANCE WITH A BOY
WHEN YOU'VE ONLY DANCED WITH SOME GIRL.

I WONDER IF MY BRAIN
WOULD JUST KINDA BLUR
IF I SAW A "HIM" THERE
INSTEAD OF A HER.
I WONDER HOW IT IS TO DANCE WITH A BOY
WHEN YOU'VE ONLY DANCED WITH SOME GIRL.

I DO ALL THE STEPS THAT THEY DO
EXCEPT
FOR A FEW
EXCEPT
WELL, IT'S TRUE
EXCEPT

I HAVEN'T UP TILL NOW
BEEN ASKED BY A BOY
BUT JUST BEING ASKED IS A THING I'D ENJOY.
SOMETIMES I JUST VISUALIZE
ME BE'N KISSED BY HIS EYES.
HOLY SMOKE, HOLY COW

I WONDER HOW IT IS.
I WONDER HOW IT IS TO DANCE.

GIRLS.

I WONDER IF MY BRAIN
WOULD ALL KINDA BLUR-UR-UR-UR
IF I SAW A HIM THERE
INSTEAD OF A HER.

(The BACK WALL of the luncheonette flies out as the TABLES and SODA FOUNTAIN go off on each side.)

HOLY SMOKE
HOLY COW
I WONDER HOW IT IS.

(The MUSIC underscoring starts after the applause, at which time the BACK WALL of the shop comes in. Almost set, the Up Center and Right TABLES come back on. The SODA FOUNTAIN reappears from the Left. KAFRITZ *enters the soda shop along with some young* KNICKERBOCKER GREYS.)

KAFRITZ. Say, who here wants to read VALLEY OF THE DOLLS? I can get you my mother's copy for ten cents a day. *(There are no takers. She spots* GILBERT *standing Downstage of the Right table and goes to her.)* You know, Gil, it wouldn't be easy, but I might be able to get you a date for the "happening"—for a consideration.

GILBERT. *(Sits Left of the table.)* Go away, will you?

KAFRITZ. I'd go myself, but I don't neck. My mother said if I didn't neck until I was eighteen she'd buy me a Mustang. But that wouldn't be a problem for you and your dopey friend.

GILBERT. *(Digs around for a coin in one of her loafers.)* Here!

KAFRITZ. What's that for?

(VAL *is seen coming from Up Left, wearing a coolie hat and carrying a shopping bag.)*

GILBERT. A nickel to shut up and leave me alone!

(KAFRITZ *takes the nickel and clears Left a few steps.* LORI *and* CHRIS *leave.)*

VAL. *(Down Center.)* Ching-ming-ting? (GILBERT *turns her back to* VAL.) Ching-ming-ting-ting! That means: Me so solly, Princess Silverbells!

(VAL *holds out a second coolie hat,* GILBERT *turns around.)*

GILBERT. *(Rises and goes to* VAL. *Takes hat.)* Say, these are cool. Where did you get them?

VAL. The Chinese Bazaar.

GILBERT. Ah, ching-ting-ching-ting-toy!

VAL. Ah, ching-ming-ching-Myrna Loy! And look! (*Takes a scrapbook from the bag.*) The Bible! (KAFRITZ *goes Right toward the table.* VAL *takes out a magazine.*) And here's a magazine that tells all about where he lives at 62nd and Third and where he goes every day and everything!

KAFRITZ. They ought to invite you two to a nut-in! (*She retreats Down Left to the soda fountain.*)

VAL. You know the first thing I think we should do!

GILBERT. What?

VAL. Write our first love letters to each other.

GILBERT. How do you mean?

VAL. (*Bringing out notebooks from the bag, along with pencils. Gives notebook and pencil to* GILBERT.) Well, I'll write to him and you be him and write to me.

GILBERT. Say, that's a good idea.

VAL. Okay, how's this: "O Great Lover of the Orient!"

GILBERT. Oh, that's a very good start, Val. Now I'm Henry writing to you: (*Writes.*) "O most beautiful and glamorous love-kitten!"

VAL. Eeeeeeek!

GILBERT. "Your eyes are twin sins."

VAL. "It was a night of love that I will never forget if I live to be a thousand!"

(*At this,* TWO BOY'S *heads come around slowly. The* GIRLS *giggle. The* TWO BOYS *look at each other. Brother! The* GIRLS *continue to write.*)

RUSS. Ho, boy! (*To* HAL.) Do you know those girls?

HAL. No, but I'm already crazy about 'em! (*Crosses Left to* KAFRITZ.) Hey, Kaf!

(RUSS *follows* HAL.)

KAFRITZ. Got a problem, soldier?

RUSS. Are you still fixing dates for the dance?

KAFRITZ. (*Rises.*) For a consideration, of course.

RUSS. (*Points to the* GIRLS *at the Right table.*) What about those two chicks?

KAFRITZ. (*Sees who they are.*) Oh-oh!

HAL. What do you mean, oh-oh?

KAFRITZ. Those might run you a little higher.

HAL. Higher than what?

KAFRITZ. Those are two very exclusive debutantes.

RUSS. Well, we don't have much dough!

VAL. (*Writing.*) "Till the sands of the desert run cold, from your own little passion flower."

GILBERT. "From your adoring Henry in heavenly memory of one glorious night of love."

RUSS. (*He and* HAL *turn together to* KAFRITZ.) Name it.

KAFRITZ. Make it five bucks.

(RUSS *hands over the money.*)

VAL. (*Reading the magazine.*) Say, we're going to have to hurry if we're going to follow him today!

GILBERT. What's it say?

VAL. It says he has lunch every Friday at Flynn's Fish Haven on Lexington. We can follow him then.

GILBERT. (*Gathering stuff together.*) We can paste this stuff in later.

KAFRITZ. (*Sauntering up to* VAL *and* GILBERT, *all smiles.*) I think I've got it worked out for you, kids.

VAL. Well, if it isn't the singing nun!

VAL and GIL. Ah, ching-ting-ming. (*They bow once to her mockingly.*)

GILBERT. Mean old Chinese curse: May you have mouthful peanut butter and no milk.

(*Both* VAL *and* GILBERT *beat a hasty retreat.*)

RUSS. (*To* KAFRITZ.) Boy, are YOU a fixer!

KAFRITZ. (*Grimly.*) Take it easy, will you? I've just started! Wait here! (*She runs out.*)

RUSS. Well, how do you like that?

HAL. And with our dough!

RUSS. Come on!

(*The* TWO BOYS *start to leave.*)

KENNY. Mills, St. James, Fall in!

(HAL *and* RUSS *stop.*)

HAL. But that girl's got our five bucks, Kenny!

KENNY. I said, fall in, soldier!

(RUSS *and* HAL *fall in, walk Down Center towards* KENNY *and look at each other in distress.*)

HAL. What do you think?

RUSS. That's my whole allowance!

HAL. Let's go!

(*Both* HAL *and* RUSS *run out of the shop as fast as they can.*)

KENNY. Doggone it, Russ, halt! (*He runs to the door, but they've gone. Comes back.*) Whitney, Vanderbilt, Stuyvesant! Mikolanvitch!

(*The* SOLDIERS *fall in line.*)

MEN. Yes, sir.
KENNY. This is Operation Search and Seize Deserters! About face! Forward—March! Hup 2 3 4! Hup 2 3 4! Hup 2 3 4!

(*They march out. The remainder of the* GIRLS *follow them as the SCENERY flies out and the TABLES and SODA FOUNTAIN move off.*)

BLACKOUT

ACT ONE

SCENE 9

Telephone Booth. Stage Right we see a telephone booth. On the Left side of the Stage, near some buildings are two garbage cans. STELLA *enters from Left and sneaks across Stage, still heavily veiled. A few moments later,* ORIENT *appears from Left, following her. He stops Center, turns Upstage and lowers his head when he sees a* MAN *coming from Right, carrying golf clubs. The* GOLFER *exits Left, and* ORIENT *continues to follow* STELLA *Right. At this moment,* KAFRITZ *enters Up Right and flattens herself against a building, while the two GARBAGE CANS rise and cross Center.* ORIENT *stops. The GARBAGE CANS stop and rest on the ground again.* ORIENT *exits and the GARBAGE CANS again walk toward Right.* KAFRITZ *stops them.*

KAFRITZ. (*Removing the lids.*) I wonder what Miss Cooney would say if she heard that two of her very nice young ladies were following an old man all over town in the middle of the night.

(*Out come* GILBERT *and* VAL.)

GILBERT. All right, how much? (*Starts to take money from her shoe.*)
KAFRITZ. No, I tell you what I'll do. (*Puts lids back on.*) If you'll go to this Knickerbocker Greys thing with a couple of cute

boys I know, I won't tell. And I'll even cut the price for you—a buck and a quarter.

VAL. She's all heart, isn't she?

(*Both* VAL *and* GILBERT *speak in Chinese and run around* KAFRITZ.)

KAFRITZ. Or would you rather I tell everybody where you go every afternoon at three?

(*They stop Down Right.*)

GILBERT. (*Puzzled.*) What's she talking about?

KAFRITZ. She has to go to a shrink, that's what I'm talking about!

GILBERT. A shrink?

KAFRITZ. A head doctor, stupid, for when you're going crazy or something.

GILBERT. (*Crossing to* KAFRITZ.) If you aren't the meanest, nastiest—

VAL. No, wait. If she knows that much, maybe we ought to tell her the whole truth.

KAFRITZ. (*Suspiciously.*) What whole truth?

VAL. I mean why I go to Doctor Leary. You see—I'm a junk eater.

KAFRITZ. A what?

GILBERT. She's hooked on SOB.

VAL. I have to take a trip every afternoon.

KAFRITZ. But that's illegal—especially near a school!

GILBERT. (*Returns to* VAL.) She's got to expand her mind, or she'd go stark raving mad.

VAL. But I missed it this afternoon. His shade was up. That meant he didn't have any.

GILBERT. That's his signal. When he's got some he pulls his shade down.

VAL. (*Groping.*) Gil! (*Wanders toward Center.*) Are the lights going out?

GILBERT. (*Taking her hand.*) Here I am, dear. Don't be afraid.

VAL. My extremities are growing numb. (*Starts Right.*)

GILBERT. (*Going with* VAL, *Downstage of her.*) That's this monkey on her back.

VAL. Will you take me there, please, before it's too late.

GILBERT. Of course, dear. (*Leading her off Right.*) We'll pick up some morphine on the way just to hold you.

(*They exit, leaving* KAFRITZ *glaring after them, unable to decide whether she's been taken or not.* RUSS *and* HAL *run on from Left.*)

HAL. Kafritz! What about that five bucks?

KALFRITZ. How can you talk about five bucks at a time like this? (*She goes to the telephone booth, drops a dime in the phone and dials the operator.*) Hello . . . Give me the police. . . . Police? Drug department, please. Drug department? I'd like to report a cat pushing drugs near the Norton School—an apartment at 62nd and Third. His signal is, if he's got it, he pulls down the shade. Be on the lookout for a couple of addicts from the school that are on the way there now . . . No, not me. I'm the connection. (*She hangs up, checks the coin return slot for her dime, then looks at the* BOYS *significantly.*)

RUSS. We'd better call out the troops!

(*The* BOYS *run off Left as* KAFRITZ *comes out of the booth.*)

KAFRITZ. (*Coming Down Center.*) There! I did it! (*Sings.*)

I OFTEN HAVE THESE MISERABLE INSTINCTS
BUT I ENDEAVOR TO RESIST 'EM
BY CLENCHIN' MY FIST 'N
BY KICKIN' MY SHOE HARD
I TRY, BUT NOT TOO HARD.

SHE WAS OUT TO GET ME
BUT I GOT HER FIRST.
WHEN SHE GOT MALIC-IOUS—SHE
HAPPENED TO PICK A KID
COULD BE JUST AS VIC-I-OUS
AND TWICE AS VIN-DICATIVE.
I AM ROUGH AND I AM RUTHLESS
THOUGH IT'S TOUGH
THE BITTER TRUTH IS—

NOBODY STEPS ON KAFRITZ.
IF THEY DO THEN THEY MUST BE CRUSHED.
MOST OF THE WORLD ARE HALF-WITS
AND THEIR LAUGHTER WILL SOON BE HUSHED.
A SUPERIOR MENTAL I.Q.
MAKES INFERIOR MINDS DISLIKE YOU.
IF THE WORLD STARTS A RUCKUS
WHERE ALL OF THEM RUN A-MUCK IS
TO STEP ON KAFRITZ.

MY FRIENDS, YOU'RE NEVER TOO YOUNG TO BE
ROTTEN
NEVER TOO YOUNG TO BE DOWNRIGHT DIRTY
THOUGH I'M NOT A STINKER YET
I'M A FIRST CLASS STINKERETTE.

NEVER TOO YOUNG TO BE HOSTILE
NEVER TOO YOUNG TO BE JUST PLAIN CRUMMY
YOU CAN CATCH ON IN A WINK
BE A RAT
BE A FINK
I'M A MONSTER, I AM MISER'BLE
AND I'M GLAD IT'S PLAINLY VISIBLE.

NOBODY STEPS ON KAFRITZ
IF THEY DO THEN THEY MUST BE CRUSHED.
OUT OF MY WAY YOU HALF-WITS
NOBODY STEPS ON KAFRITZ!

BLACKOUT

ACT ONE

Scene 10

Orient's Apt. Exterior and Interior. VAL *and* GILBERT *run in from Upstage checking house numbers. They stop in front of Henry's apartment and kneel.*

GILBERT. This is it!

VAL. Eeek! (*She falls to her knees and salaams.*) BANZAI!

GILBERT. (*After a moment, does the same.*) Shalom! Do you remember what a drag everything was until we found our true mission in life?

VAL. Yeah, things are sure different now. (*Sings.*)
HENRY, SWEET HENRY
SINCE I ADORE YOU, HENRY
I'M ALL CHILLS AND THRILLS AND BUTTERFLIES.
YOUR CRAZY MUSIC TRULY TICKLES US

GILBERT.
ALTHOUGH YOUR WHOLE TECHNIQUE'S REE-DICK-EL-US.

VAL.
SOME LOVE VAN CLIBURN
BUT MY SWEET HENRY, I YEARN
JUST TO HEAR YOUR GOLDEN MELODIES.
I LOVE YOU ASTRONOMICALLY

GILBERT.
THO' YOU'VE CRACKED UP HARMONICALLY.

BOTH.
MY SWEET HENRY, SWEET HENRY
I LOVE YOU.

(VAL, *in her excitement, turns a somersault, then reaches for the Bible, lies flat on her back, puts her legs straight up in the air and puts the Bible on her feet.*)

GILBERT.
YOU LOOK LIKE A WOMAN IN LOVE TO ME,
FLUTTERING PULSE, MOISTURING BROW
HANDS THAT ARE CLAMMY AND TREM-B-LING.

VAL. Wow!

GILBERT.
YOU LOOK LIKE A WOMAN IN LOVE TO ME
HEAD ERECT BUT SHOULDERS THAT SHOW THE STRAIN
AND THERE'S THE CHIN, RIGID AND TAUT.

VAL.
GOLLY, IT SHOWS EVEN MORE THAN I THOUGHT.

GILBERT.
MY TRAINED EYE CAN SEE, INDUBITABLY
YOU LOOK LIKE A WOMAN IN LOVE TO ME.

BOTH.
HENRY, SWEET HENRY
SINCE I ADORE YOU, HENRY
I'M ALL CHILLS AND THRILLS AND BUTTERFLIES
BECAUSE I LOVE YOU ASTRONOMICALLY.
THO' YOU'VE CRACKED UP HARMONICALLY
MY SWEET HENRY, SWEET HENRY, I LOVE
HENRY SWEET HENRY, I LOVE
HENRY SWEET HENRY, I LOVE YOU.

(*At the end of the song,* VAL *and* GILBERT *remain on the Down Left fire escape as ORIENT'S APARTMENT moves down into position. Stairs, Left, lead from the street to Orient's building. Downstage of the stairs is a large bay window with three windows facing the street. The entrance to the apartment is Up Left. On this door, there are five locks. On the same wall, to the Right, is a large arch, filled with a beaded curtain. In front of the bay window is a small cabinet which* ORIENT *uses as a bar. In the Center of the room is a chaise filled with pillows. On the Right wall is a window, Downstage of which is a large pillow ottoman. It is still dark.* KAFRITZ *and her cronies come on Down Right. She peers up at* VAL, *follows the direction of* VAL'S *gaze and moves across the street with her friends, now staring at Orient's apartment. A few* PASSERS-BY *note this and stop to stare themselves. Finally there is quite a group of people looking at Orient's apartment and at each other. They are a bit embarrassed by this activity and some turn to explain to the audience. A* LADY, *carrying a bag of groceries, stops in front of Orient's apartment when she notices* EVERYONE *staring at the building.*)

ENSEMBLE.
WE ARE WATCHING PEOPLE WATCHING.
WE ARE PEOPLE WATCHING PEOPLE
THOUGH WE DON'T KNOW WHAT WE'RE WATCHING
WE MUST WATCH THE PEOPLE WATCHING.

WE ARE WATCHING PEOPLE WATCHING.
WE ARE PEOPLE WATCHING PEOPLE
THOUGH WE DON'T KNOW WHAT WE'RE WATCHING
WE MUST WATCH THE PEOPLE WATCHING.

TENOR.
NOT THAT WE ARE NOSEY
I MUST MAKE THAT PERFECTLY CLEAR.
BUT BECAUSE IT'S NONE OF OUR BUSINESS
IS PRECISELY WHY WE'RE HERE.

PEOPLE WATCHING PEOPLE
PEOPLE WATCHING PEOPLE
WATCHING PEOPLE WATCHING.

WE ARE PEOPLE WATCHING PEOPLE
THOUGH WE DON'T KNOW WHAT WE'RE WATCHING
WE MUST WATCH THE PEOPLE WATCHING.

I'M A NATURAL WATCHER.
WATCHING PEOPLE IS A KICK TO ME.
BOTH MY DAD AND MOTHER WERE FRENCH
AND WATCHING PEOPLE WAS THEIR HOBBY.

PEOPLE WATCHING PEOPLE
PEOPLE WATCHING PEOPLE
PEOPLE WATCHING PEOPLE.

(ORIENT *and* STELLA *have entered through the back window of*

Orient's apartment. STELLA *collapses on the floor near the window;* ORIENT *climbs in and goes to turn off the lights.*)

ENSEMBLE. OHHHHHHHHH!

HENRY. Alone at last. (*They embrace. He kisses her through the veil. Gets veil caught in mouth.*) Now, may I suggest that you go in there and divest yourself of that shroud?

(*With a few suitably modest moans she exits into what must surely be the bedroom.* HENRY *nips quickly to his door and locks one after the other five locks on his apartment door, and then disappears around the corner into a dressing room. The* KNICKERBOCKER GREYS *enter Right.*)

KENNY.
HUT 2 3 4
HUT 2 3 4
HUT 2 3 4

COLUMN RIGHT RIGHT!

HALT 2 3 HUT

PRESENT ARMS HUT	ENSEMBLE. WE ARE WATCHING PEOPLE WATCHING.
LEFT FACE MARK TIME MARK	WE ARE PEOPLE WATCHING PEOPLE THOUGH WE DON'T KNOW WHAT WE'RE WATCHING
WHITNEY, VANDERBILT—FORWARD ESCAPES	WE MUST WATCH THE PEOPLE WATCHING.
ST. JAMES, MILLS — THE REAR MARCH	PEOPLE WATCHING PEOPLE PEOPLE WATCHING PEOPLE
ROSS, STUYVESANT—LEFT FLANK	PEOPLE WATCHING PEOPLE PEOPLE WATCHING PEOPLE
HUT HUT	PEOPLE WATCHING PEOPLE.
DOUBLE TIME	(*A* POLICEMAN *enters carrying guns.*)

HA, HA, HA, HA OHHHHHHHH!
HA, HA, HA, HA

(ORIENT, *resplendent in a showy dressing gown, bounds out of his dressing room, spraying the room with perfume.*)

ORIENT. (*Sings.*)
FOREVER, I SHALL WORSHIP YOU
MY STELLA, DEAR,
FOREVER
YES FOREVER AND A DAY BEYOND
MY HEART WILL . . .
(*In the middle of this,* STELLA *emerges timidly as the MUSIC swells to a passionate climax. She is dressed like Margaret Sullivan in a white pajama top but has neglected to remove her black hat with the veils and her long black gloves and still clutches her purse. He leaps to embrace her again, but she slithers past him and crouches on the sofa shaking with nervousness and whimpering a bit.*) Oh, my precious pearl of great price!
STELLA. (*Sings.*)
HENRY, SWEET HENRY
YOU FINALLY TRIUMPHED, HENRY
I CAN FIGHT NO LONGER.
ORIENT. (*Goes to her.*)
I LOVE YOU WITH SUCH A PASSION
IN MY BRAIN ARE CYMBALS CRASHING.

(*She runs away from him, around the chaise. He follows. They* BOTH *sit on the sofa.*)

STELLA. C-c-could I have a drink first?
ORIENT. But of course, darling! What more beautiful overture to the symphony of love than a belt or two of the grape! Name it, macushla!
STELLA. White mint?
ORIENT. White mint! (*He stops.*) White mint?
STELLA. White mint.
ORIENT. White mint. (*Goes to the bar and starts looking for white mint.*) I'll be a son-of-a-bitch!

(*Outside the* CROWD *has begun to stir again.*)

HOT DOG MAN. Hot dogs!

ENSEMBLE.	WALLACE.
WE ARE WATCHING PEOPLE WATCHING.	LA, LA, LA, LA, LA, LA, LA, etc.)

WE ARE PEOPLE WATCHING PEOPLE	
THOUGH WE DON'T KNOW WHAT WE'RE WATCHING	HAWKERS.
WE MUST WATCH THE PEOPLE WATCHING.	Hot dogs! Balloons!

ENSEMBLE.
LA, LA, LA, LA, LA, LA, LA, LA, LA, LA
LA, LA, LA, LA, LA, LA, LA, LA, LA, LA
LA, LA, LA, LA, LA, LA, LA, LA, LA, LA
LA, LA, LA, LA, LA, LA, LA, LA, LA, LA

PEOPLE WATCHING
PEOPLE WATCHING
PEOPLE WATCHING
PEOPLE WATCHING.
(*By now,* ORIENT *has given up finding any white mint. Instead he pours from another bottle, takes the glass with him and turns off the LIGHTS.*)
OHHHHHHHH!

ORIENT. I knew I had it someplace. (HENRY *slides onto the sofa beside* STELLA.) Sip, sweet.

(*But at this first touch, she is galvanized into hysterical action, seizing him in a clutch of manic strength, one arm about his neck.*)

STELLA. Oh, darling!

ORIENT. (*Choking.*) You're hurting my throat, sweet!

STELLA. I'm so scared!

ORIENT. My windpipe, sweet—you're hurting it!

STELLA. (*With a deathgrip on him.*) Be gentle with me, please!

ORIENT. God damn it, darling, you're choking me! (*As he manages to free himself, she leaps to her feet and sits on the ottoman Right, a frightened fawn.* ORIENT *massages his throat Left of the sofa.*) Don't you know you could kill somebody like that?

STELLA. P-p-play something—will you?

ORIENT. I will, dear—afterward. (*She moans as he approaches her.*) Don't you trust me, mavourneen?

STELLA. Of course! But somebody might see us! The window!

(*He is about to pull down the window shade when he looks out the window and up to the fire-escape Down Left, where* VAL *and* GILBERT *are sitting.*)

GILBERT and VAL. Look, it's him!

(*They jump to their feet and make deep Oriental bows to him, jabbering Chinese all the time.* HENRY, *aghast, falls to the floor Left of the sofa.*)

STELLA. (*Rises from the ottoman.*) What? What is it?
ORIENT. Those Goddamn little punks! Those same little punks! What the hell is this?
STELLA. What little punks?
ORIENT. In the park and at the concert! Are they following us?
STELLA. Oh, my God, child detectives! (*Falls to the floor, Right of the sofa.*)
ORIENT. Detectives?
STELLA. Oh, that's George, all right! That's exactly what he would think of, little girl private eyes!
ORIENT. But that's despicable—using innocent little children to catch your wife in the sack.
STELLA. Play something, Henry, quick!
ORIENT. (*Rises.*) This is no time for music, kid. (*Starting Upstage.*) I'm going to get my pants on. (*At the door.*) You better get yours on, too.
STELLA. But the window! They might see!
ORIENT. Oh, for God's sake!

(*Back in the room, pulling his pants on, he staggers to the window and pulls the shade down, whereupon the street explodes into action. SIRENS go off, COMMANDS are shouted, GUNS are brought into the open. A* POLICEMAN *points and the barricades are knocked over.* ORIENT *stands horrified, finally puts his hands up in the air.*)

STELLA. (*Kneels Right of the sofa and begins to pray.*) Oh, my God, they've dropped it! Our father who art in heaven. . . .

(*Outside, the* GREYS *and the* COPS *collide at the entrance to the building and there is a traffic jam.* ORIENT *hobbles Right, above the sofa, still trying to put on his pants. In the meantime,* STELLA *has finished her prayer. She stands, but immediately falls to the floor in a dead faint. In the street, one* POLICEMAN *finally frees himself from the* KNICKERBOCKER GREYS *and runs up the steps and into the building. We hear him pounding on the door.*)

COP. Okay, buster, open up!
ORIENT. Will you for God's sake let me get my pants on!
COP. We're coming in! (*The* COP *begins shooting the locks off*

one by one. ORIENT *tries to pull* STELLA *to the window in hope of their both escaping. He gives up trying to get her out and decides that he'd better leave anyway, but the* COP *now has the five locks shot off. The door is kicked in and* ORIENT *stops in the window at the sight of the gun pointed at him.*) O. K., buster, don't make a move . . . (*Crosses to* ORIENT *as:*)

CURTAIN

ACT TWO

SCENE 1

Hotel Living Room. MR. BOYD *sits with the phone in his lap, trying to think of who else to call. He is commonplace enough in appearance but he happens to be a gentleman.* MRS. BOYD *is restless with sullen resentment.*

MRS. BOYD. A more disastrous homecoming I could scarcely imagine.

MR. BOYD. Did you try Dr. Greentree?

MRS. BOYD. She hasn't seen her in weeks. First Valerie and then you—

MR. BOYD. (*Dialing.*) There must be SOMEBODY at that school—

MRS. BOYD. The truth is, she's a cold, selfish, ungrateful child and this is our thanks for sending her to the best schools, the best shops in New York—

MR. BOYD. How did she look?

MRS. BOYD. Like Orphan Annie as usual. And then suddenly you're too tired to go to the Shelton party—we might just as well have stayed in Greece.

(*He has been waiting for an answer at the school but now he hangs up. A* COP *enters Down Left.*)

COP. Mr. Boyd?

MR. BOYD. Yes?

MRS. BOYD. (*Turns.*) Now what? (*The* COP *motions for* VAL *and* GILBERT *to follow him into the room.*) Welcome home. And about time, too!

VAL. (*Goes Right.*) I'm sorry.

MRS. BOYD. And where on earth did you get those silly hats?

(*Those beautiful hats that they had put on so happily, with such pride, those gay symbols of that exciting new world they were creating for themselves—silly! Crushed,* VAL *takes hers off, goes to the coffee table and throws it down on the table.*)

MR. BOYD. What's this all about, Officer?

COP. Somebody turned in a bum rap on some poor guy on Third Avenue. There was a little commotion and we picked these two up in the middle of it.

MR. BOYD. Are there any charges?

COP. No. Just keep her off the streets at night and she'll be all right. Night, Val.

VAL. Night, sir.

COP. (*Goes* L. *few steps.*) Come on, Marian.

GILBERT. (*Crossing to him.*) Good night, O Princess Cherry Blossom.

VAL. (*As they kowtow.*) Good night, O, Princess Silver Bells.

COP. I don't know. Maybe I'm crazy!

(*He and* GILBERT *exit.* VAL *shucks out of her coat and throws it and the Bible on a chair.*)

MR. BOYD. What did you do, kid, rob a bank? (*Holds out his arms.*)

(*To point up her superiority to* VAL *in orderliness,* MRS. BOYD *straightens the coat on the chair and picks up the Bible.*)

VAL. (*Goes to her* FATHER, *kisses him.*) Honestly, father, I don't even know what happened! I mean Gil and I were just goofing around and we forgot what time it was, we really did, and then BOOM!—up popped about a million police and they grabbed us and we didn't even know what had happened!

MRS. BOYD. And who, may I ask, is Mr. Henry Orient? (*She has opened the Bible, seen the picture from the magazine, and is still running through the compositions.*)

VAL. (*With a gasp.*) That's mine!

MRS. BOYD. Just a moment, Valerie.

VAL. (*Frantic.*) But you've got no right to that, it's mine.

MRS. BOYD. Now, Valerie.

MR. BOYD. Now, take it easy, dear.

VAL. (*Goes to* MR. BOYD.) Gil and I have this secret and a secret is sacred, isn't it, Father?

MR. BOYD. If it's their secret, Iz—

MRS. BOYD. Look, Frank. (*Rises from sofa.*) It's not only that she's been brought home by the police, apparently for running around the streets like a little tart, but I'd like to hear some of this.

VAL. (*Almost choking, she follows* MRS. BOYD.) Please don't read it, Mother! Please don't.

MRS. BOYD. (*Going Downstage.*) "O, most beautiful and glamorous love kitten!"

VAL. I'll do something!

MRS. BOYD. And how do you like this? "Your eyes are twin sins!"

VAL. (*Sobbing, a few steps Upstage.*) It's supposed to be a secret.

MR. BOYD. I wouldn't go on if I were you, Iz.

MRS. BOYD. And this is how it's signed: (*Takes the Bible to* MR. BOYD.) "From your adoring Henry in heavenly memory of one glorious night of love."

MR. BOYD. (*Angrily. Takes Bible and throws it on the Left chair.*) For God's sake, that's enough, Iz!

VAL. But it's just pretend, it wasn't real, it's just pretend.

MRS. BOYD. (*Goes toward* VAL.) And now I want to know who this Mr. Henry Orient is.

VAL. Why did you ever come back? Why don't you go away and stay away!

MR. BOYD. Now, stop that, Valerie!

MRS. BOYD. Are you going to tell me who this man is or not?

VAL. I was just fooling before but I'm not now, not any more. Now I'm really going to him! (*She runs off Left.*)

MR. BOYD. Valerie! (*Turns on* MRS. BOYD.) Of all the idiotic, stupid— (*Exits Left.*)

BLACKOUT

ACT TWO

SCENE 2

As the Boyd LIVING ROOM slides off, the WASHINGTON SQUARE set comes in and we find VAL *all alone, sitting on a bench, Right. The* HIPPIES *enter Left. There is another bench Left.*

HIPPIES.

WEARY NEAR TO DYIN'
STUMBLIN' THRU THE DARK
WANDERIN' AND SEARCHIN'
FOR THE HUMAN SPARK.

HEAVY IS THE BURDEN
WEARY IS THE HEART
WHEN THE LOVE WITHIN YOU
YOU CANNOT IMPART.

VAL.

WEARY NEAR TO DYIN'
STUMBLIN' THRU THE DARK
ALL MY LIFE I'LL WANDER
FIFTH AVENUE AND PARK.

HEAVY IS THE BURDEN
WEARY IS THE HEART

WHEN YOU'VE GOT A MOTHER
SAYS THAT YOU'RE A TART.

HIPPIES.
BOOP BOOP
BOOP BOOP

MEN.	LADIES.
OOH WAH OOH	BOOP BOOP
OOH WAH OOH	BOOP BOOP

MEN.
RAMA RAMA RAMA
MAMA GURU GURU
LA LA LA LA LA LA LA
LO LO LULULULU

BOO BEE BOO

LADIES.
BEEP BOOP BOOP

MEN.
ZEE BEE ZEE

LADIES.
BEEP BOOP BOOP

MEN.
WAH OPE

LADIES.
BEEP

MEN.
WAH OPE

LADIES.
BEEP

MEN.
OOH WUP

LADIES.
BEEP

MEN.
OOH WUP

LADIES.
BEEP

MEN.
ZEE BEE ZEE

LADIES.
BEEP BOOP BOOP

MEN.
ZEE BEE ZEE

LADIES.
BEEP BOOP BOOP

(VAL *takes a piece of rose-colored gelatin from* PAUL, *a dancing Hippie.*)

ALL HIPPIES.
AHHHHHHHH. . . . .

PAUL. (*Screams.*) Aaaahhhhhh!

(VAL *notices that* PAUL *is in agony. When she returns the gelatin to him, he is happy again and continues to dance.*)

HIPPIES.
BOOP BOOP BOOP BOOP
BOOP BOOP BOOP BOOP

(TRAMP *enters, takes cigarette from a* HIPPIE.)

MEN.
WAH OPE

LADIES.
BEEP

MEN.
WAH OPE

LADIES.
BEEP

MEN.
OOH WUP

LADIES.
BEEP

MEN.
OOH WUP

LADIES.
BEEP

(TRAMP *smokes and dances.*)

HIPPIES.
BOOP BOOP BOOP BOOP
BOOP BOOP BOOP BOOP

(ALL HIPPIES *run or crawl to the Right park bench where a* WORKMAN *is eating a banana, the end of his lunch.* VAL *is seated next to him. Both the* WORKMAN *and* VAL *escape the mob by standing on the bench. The* WORKMAN *finally throws the banana skin high in the air.* ALL HIPPIES *search for it on the ground.* ONE HIPPIE *retrieves it, holds it high in the air as the* OTHERS *return to their own little world. In adoration to the banana skin:*)

AAAAAAAAAAAAHHHHHHHHHHHH!

(*A* GIRL *with a feather comes Down Center and dances. A* HIPPIE *runs on from Left, whistles to the others. They gather around, and on, the benches and sing:)*

AH AH AH AH AH

AH AH AH AH AH

(*A* POLICEMAN *has entered and is amazed to note the peace and calm of the group. The* TRAMP *comes through the arch and the* POLICEMAN *grabs him and pulls him off Left.*)

WEARY NEAR TO DYIN'

AAAAAAAAAHHHHHHHH

STUMBLIN' THRU THE DARK

AAAAAAAAAAAHHHHHHHHH

WANDERIN' AND SEARCHIN'

WAH OOP WAH OOP

HEAVY IS THE BURDEN

AAAAAAAAAAHHHHHHHHH

WEARY IS THE HEART

(VAL *exits through arch and off Left.*)

AAAAAAAAAAHHHHHHHHHHH

WHEN THE LOVE WITHIN YOU

WAH OOP WAH OOP

WAH OOP WAH OOP

WAH YAH YAH YAH WAH

YAH YAH YAH WAH. . . . .

BLACKOUT

ACT TWO

Scene 3

ORIENT'S APARTMENT moves Downstage. Our hero is in a dazzling dressing gown gorgeously initialed. He is singing with the happiness of a man who has a female in the bedroom, and he is projecting his song in that direction as he screws on the last of the five locks that were shot off.

Orient. (*Singing.*)
FOREVER
I SHALL WORSHIP YOU, MY VALERIE.
FOREVER
YES FOREVER AND A DAY BEYOND.
MY HEART WILL VOW AGAIN
THE VOW IT MADE YOU THEN
THE VERY MOMENT WHEN
IT VOWED FOREVER.
(*The PHONE rings and as he answers it we pick up* Mrs. Boyd *in the hotel.*) Whoever you may be, I wish you nought but happiness!

Mrs. Boyd. Mr. Henry ORIENT?

Orient. (*A female voice!*) It is indeed, and what music you have poured into those humble syllables—

Mrs. Boyd. This is Mrs. Frank Boyd.

Orient. And how may I serve you, my dear Mrs. Boyd—?

Mrs. Boyd. I would like to speak to my daughter.

Orient. (*When he can speak.*) May we have that again?

Mrs. Boyd. I would like to speak to my daughter Valerie.

Orient. You're—Valerie's—mother?

Mrs. Boyd. I am.

Orient. (*Dazed.*) Valerie? (*Cupping the phone.*) Just a moment, please.

(*Wearing only a towel, a* Dish *sticks her head in.*)

Valerie. You rang, maestro?

Orient. (*Goes toward her.*) It's your mother.

Valerie. (*In astonishment.*) From Poland?

Orient. (*Pulls phone away from her.*) YOU speak to her.

Valerie. In what language?

Orient. English—

Valerie. That's not my mom!

(*She disappears and he returns to the phone uneasily.*)

ORIENT. There would seem to be a little misunderstanding here, Mrs. Boyd. She says she's not your mother—

MRS. BOYD. Do you know how old Valerie is, Mr. Orient?

ORIENT. No, I can't say that I do—

MRS. BOYD. Fourteen.

ORIENT. (*When he can speak.*) Fourteen—YEARS?

MRS. BOYD. She is fourteen years old and that's all I'd have to tell the police—

ORIENT. Now just a moment, Mrs. Boyd. Let's not lose our heads—

MRS. BOYD. Then will you call her to the phone?

ORIENT. Of course! (*Cupping the phone, few steps Upstage.*) Valerie!

VALERIE. You wish to play wiz me, cheri?

ORIENT. How old are you?

VALERIE. (*Flipping the towel gaily near window.*) What you theenk, M'sieur!

ORIENT. (*Goes Right, above sofa.*) Will you for God's sake cut that out and tell me how old you are?

VALERIE. (*Straight.*) What is all this?

ORIENT. (*Too agitated to think clearly.*) She says you're only fourteen—

VALERIE. Who the hell is this broad?

MRS. BOYD. Mr. Orient—

ORIENT. (*In phone.*) Just a moment, Mrs. Broad. (*To* VALERIE.) She's got it in her nut that you're her fourteen-year-old daughter—

VALERIE. (*Few steps Left.*) You mean you're mixed up with some fourteen-year-old kid?

ORIENT. Oh, for God's sake, no—

VALERIE. Then how'd she get your number?

MRS. BOYD. (*Hearing her voice.*) Isn't that Valerie?

ORIENT. (*Goes Left.*) By rather an amusing coincidence it is, but this one's not your daughter—

VALERIE. (*Following him.*) That's pretty sick, you know, sloshing around with that fourteen-year-old stuff—

ORIENT. (*In phone.*) This Valerie happens to be an old family friend from the—Peace Corps—

VALERIE. (*At window.*) I mean I was fourteen myself once and let me tell you, buster, I could write a book about creeps like you—

ORIENT. But I've never even seen this kid—

VALERIE. Then why don't you hang up on her? (*Exits.*)

ORIENT. (*Firmly.*) Now listen, Mrs. Boyd, unless you can control yourself—

MRS. BOYD. And if you should be thinking of hanging up on me, Mr. Orient, please remember that I have only to give the police my daughter's age and your address and leave the rest to them.

ORIENT. Oh, now really, Mrs. Boyd, we wouldn't want to take a step that we might all regret, would we?

VALERIE. (*Re-enters.*) Are you going to hang up on her or not?

ORIENT. (*In phone.*) Hold it for just a moment, n'est-ce pas, will you? (*He buries the phone under a pillow.*)

VALERIE. (*Puts on slip.*) You know what I ought to do?

ORIENT. (*Crosses to her.*) Now look, sweetheart—

VALERIE. (*Goes Left.*) I ought to pull the chain on you right now! That's what I ought to do.

ORIENT. (*Soothingly.*) All you've got to do is say: Mrs. Boyd, my name is Valerie whatever-the-hell-it-is—

VALERIE. (*Crosses Downstage.*) Because you're not going to stop at fourteen, buster!

ORIENT. Val baby, please!

VALERIE. (*Backs Up Left.*) You've got your eye on a cradle—

ORIENT. (*A scream.*) Will you shut up! (*Hurriedly and dulcetly into the phone.*) Just one wee moment more, Mrs. Boyd baby— (*Goes Right above sofa.*) You rockhead, she's going to buzz for the fuzz!

VALERIE. (*Paling.*) The fuzz!

ORIENT. What the hell do you think I've been talking about?

VALERIE. Coming here?

ORIENT. Not if you speak to her—

VALERIE. (*Exiting.*) Just left, thank you!

ORIENT. (*Desperately.*) But she hasn't called yet, damnit! And she won't if she hears your voice! Once she hears your voice that'll be the end of it, don't you understand?

VALERIE. (*Off.*) Not if my voice sounds like her punk's voice—

ORIENT. (*Following her off.*) But how can you do this after what we've been to each other!

(*We hear a loud SLAP.* ORIENT *bounces back the entire length of the beaded doorway and then enters the room holding his face. Sits on the Left end of the sofa.*)

VALERIE. (*Returns. She has on a police cap and is adjusting her gear. She's a police sergeant.*) You son-of-a-bitch, I could lose my stripes for this! (*She exits through the door to the hall and then out through the door leading to the street. She walks down the steps and then off Right.*)

ORIENT. (*Stunned.*) And I've never even laid eyes on the little . . . punk! (*Now he's got it. Punk. So when he picks up the phone now,* HENRY *is himself again, and at his sultriest.*) Mrs. Boyd?

MRS. BOYD. Yes?

ORIENT. I was afraid you'd hung up and I might never again enjoy the sweet music of the loveliest voice I've ever heard in twenty years. Tell me. Does you daughter ever dress like a Chinaman?

MRS. BOYD. (*Puzzled.*) Well, she was wearing a coolie hat—

ORIENT. Then the mystery is solved, dear lady! Now, if I may make a suggestion . . .

(*As he starts his suggestions, the MUSIC swells into FOREVER and the LIGHTS fade on him as his SET is withdrawn.* MRS. BOYD, *still on the other end of the phone, listens coolly as the WALL of her living room comes into place behind her.*)

ACT TWO

SCENE 4

The Boyds' Living Room.

MRS. BOYD. (*Into phone.*) All right. I'll try.

(*She hangs up and is reflecting on the situation when* MR. BOYD *enters Left with the Bible.*)

MR. BOYD. I've been looking through this book, Iz, and believe me, this is quite a revelation. And not a very pleasant one either.

MRS. BOYD. Don't you think we might leave all that sort of interpretation to the psychiatrists?

MR. BOYD. I don't think we need one for this one. (*Moves Upstage, puts book on mantel.*) I'm going down to Police Headquarters.

MRS. BOYD. (*Picks up cup of coffee from table Downstage of armchair.*) I must say this is really something new!

MR. BOYD. New how?

MRS. BOYD. Such concern for a child you don't even believe is yours.

MR. BOYD. (*Breaks Downstage.*) What the hell has that got to do with this? This is a child in trouble—and she needs help—that's all that matters.

MRS. BOYD. (*Puts cup down.*) Oh, for God's sake, Frank, stop being melodramatic. (*Rises and goes to the mantel.*) She had a tantrum like a million other spoiled kids and she's put on this act of running away for the sole purpose of frightening her parents, (*Breaks Downstage again with a piece of paper from the notebook on the mantel.*) and once that's done, and she gets hungry, she'll be home in time for dinner.

MR. BOYD. That's not the trouble I was thinking of. But we'll go into that later. What about Mr. Orient?

MRS. BOYD. Still no answer.

(*She goes out Left, followed by* MR. BOYD.)

ACT TWO

SCENE 5

As the Boyds' LIVING ROOM slides off, the LOCKERS, reversed, to show the front of the school portal, come in. The FACTUS theme starts and the GIRLS *are heard singing coming to school.*

GIRLS. (*Offstage Right.*)
FACTUS, FACTUM, FACTU, FACTI
(GIRLS *now enter.*)
ICH BIN DU BIST
IHR SEID SIE IST
I MUST BE A MASOCHIST
MIT ICH NIN DU BIST
UND IHR SEID
I AHM COMMITTING ZOO-IZ-SEID.

(GILBERT *enters Right as the* GIRLS *continue to sing softly and trying not to notice her.*)

KAFRITZ. Is there any word yet?

GILBERT. No.

KAFRITZ. Don't worry, Gil dear. We'll find her.

GIRLS. (*Softly.*)
FACTUS, FACTUM
FACTU, FACTI
I DON'T SAY LATIN
STINKS EXACTLY
LATUS LATI LATUM TOO
I THINK THAT I—

KAFRITZ. (*She signals* GIRLS *to be quiet.*) It takes a shock like this to make us realize what a friend really means to us. We haven't been very kind to Val, none of us, and I can't deny that I'm probably the most guilty. But now that she's out there somewhere, lost in a great city, and at the mercy of the elements, the ugly truth has been brought home to us at last, and we must lift our voices in prayer that she be returned to us safely so we can make up to her for the wicked way we've treated her. (REBECCA *steps forward with her violin.* KAFRITZ *sings.*)

DON'T LET IT RAIN ON THAT POOR LITTLE PERSON
WHO IS LOST OUT THERE SOMEWHERE
IN THE CRUEL, CRUEL WORLD.

GIRLS.
DON'T LET IT RAIN, DON'T LET IT RAIN,
DON'T LET IT THUNDER
OR LIGHT'NING, THAT MIGHT BE FRIGHT'NING.
LIGHT UP THE STARS
TILL THEY'RE TWINKELELY NEON
LET THE MOON SHINE A BLOSSOMY LIGHT
IN THE SCAREY NIGHT.
THERE'S NOTHIN' WORSE 'N
A POOR LITTLE PERSON
LOST IN THE RAIN, DON'T LET IT RAIN
DON'T LET IT RAIN!

KAFRITZ.
LET'S PASS THE HAT FOR A POOR LITTLE PERSON
WHO IS LOST OUT THERE SOMEWHERE
IN THE CRUEL, CRUEL WORLD.
GIVE TILL IT HURTS, GIVE TILL IT HURTS
GET THAT COIN OUT
DON'T LET THE TORCH OF KINDNESS BOIN OUT.
A NICE FAT REWARD FOR A POOR LITTLE PERSON
AND SOME FLOWERS TO SEND TO SEND TO HER
FOLKS,

GIRLS.
TO HER LOVING FOLKS.
THERE'S NOTHIN' WORSE 'N
A POOR LITTLE PERSON
LOST IN THE RAIN, DON'T LET IT RAIN
DON'T LET IT RAIN.

(GIRLS *stop time chorus.*)
DON'T LET IT RAIN ON THAT POOR LITTLE PERSON
WHO IS LOST OUT THERE SOMEWHERE
IN THE CRUEL, CRUEL WORLD.
DON'T LET IT RAIN, DON'T LET IT RAIN
DON'T LET IT THUNDER
OR LIGHT'NING, THAT MIGHT BE FRIGHT'NING.
LIGHT UP THE STARS TILL THEY'RE TWINKELEY
NEON,
LET THE MOON SHINE A BLOSSOMY LIGHT
IN THE SCAREY NIGHT.
THERE'S NOTHIN' WORSE 'N A POOR LITTLE
PERSON
LOST IN THE RAIN, DON'T LET IT RAIN,
DON'T LET IT RAIN!

(*The* KNICKERBOCKER GREYS *come marching from Right.*)

KNICKERBOCKER GREYS.
HUP 2 3 4

HUP 2 3 4
HUP 2 3 4

GIRLS and BOYS.
DON'T LET IT RAIN ON THAT POOR LITTLE PERSON
WHO IS LOST OUT THERE SOMEWHERE
IN THE CRUEL, CRUEL WORLD.
DON'T LET IT RAIN, DON'T LET IT RAIN,
DON'T LET IT THUNDER
OR LIGHT'NING THAT MIGHT BE FRIGHT'NING.

KAFRITZ. (*Going out into the auditorium.*) Kick in, folks!

GIRLS and BOYS.
GIVE TILL IT HURTS
FOR THAT POOR LITTLE PERSON.
SEND SOME ROSES
AROUND TO HER FOLKS
TO HER GRIEVING FOLKS.
GIVE FOR A PERSON
THAT POOR LITTLE PERSON
LOST IN THE RAIN, DON'T LET IT RAIN
DON'T LET IT, DON'T LET IT RAIN
DON'T LET IT RAIN
DON'T LET IT, DON'T LET IT RAIN
DON'T LET IT RAIN
DON'T LET IT RAIN!

(*The* GIRLS *turn the lockers to the locker side. Put books in, etc.*)

THIRD GIRL. I've heard the police and the missing persons bureau and the FBI have been called in already!

FIRST GIRL. The FBI? Holy Cow!

KAFRITZ. If there was a reward for her a lot more people would go out and look.

(*The SCHOOL BELL rings.*)

LORI. Maybe she's been kidnapped by white slavers. Gangsters make millions that way.

KAFRITZ. How much do the girls make? (*The* GIRLS *leave for their classes.* KAFRITZ *stays and watches* GILBERT, *who is dejectedly hanging up her coat and is close to tears.*) What's the matter with you?

GILBERT. Go away, will you?

KAFRITZ. You know what I think? I think her parents don't want her back.

GILBERT. (*Goes to* KAFRITZ *with school bag.*) How can you talk like that when she's lost and nobody knows where she is and you're the one that started it all?

KAFRITZ. (*Smugly.*) I told you not to get in my way, didn't I? (*Goes Left, leans down to pick up her books from the bench.*) Well, maybe that'll be a little lesson to you and your crazy fat friend.

(KAFRITZ *leans down to get her books. Behind her a locker door has opened and* VAL *gives her a swift kick.* KAFRITZ *falls over the bench;* VAL *closes the locker door immediately. When* KAFRITZ *picks herself up, she is even more mystified than angry.*)

TEACHER. (*Entering Right.*) Better hurry, girls!

KAFRITZ. (*Instantaneously sweet.*) Oh, thank you so much, Miss Cooney! (*Starts to exit, then turns to* GILBERT.) You— (*Shaking her fist at* GILBERT.) crushed!

(*Exits Left.* GILBERT *starts to follow* KAFRITZ. *Once* KAFRITZ *has gone,* GILBERT *returns to* VAL'S *locker. She pulls the locker door open and* VAL *staggers out, still carrying the guitar she picked up in Washington Square.*)

VAL. (*Puts guitar on bench.*) Have you got anything to eat?

GILBERT. I've got an apple. Where've you been, for Pete's sake?

VAL. Everywhere.

GILBERT. (*Hands apple to* VAL.) Your mother's called about a zillion times.

VAL. Boy, I'll bet she's burning!

GILBERT. What happened?

VAL. You know what she said?

GILBERT. (*Kneeling on bench, picks up guitar.*) What?

VAL. She practically said I was practically a little tart.

(*MUSIC underscoring.*)

GILBERT. (*Shocked. Sits on Left end of bench.*) She really said that—to her own flesh and blood?

VAL. (*Sits Right end of bench.*) And you too!

GILBERT. But why'd she say it?

VAL. The Bible.

GILBERT. (*With a gasp.*) You mean you let her see it?

VAL. Of course not. She just grabbed it.

GILBERT. Oh, no!

VAL. Then when she read Henry's letter, that's when she really snapped.

GILBERT. (*Boiling helplessly.*) If she wasn't your mother!

VAL. That's all right—go on.

GILBERT. I mean if your own mother won't respect a secret—well, I don't know what!

VAL. She's just so dumb!

GILBERT. Gee, can't life be terrible?

VAL. Yeah! Sure can. (*Sings.*)

LIFE, OH HOW YOU'RE TREATING ME, OH LIFE
WHY DO I STRUGGLE TO SURVIVE?
WORLD, OH WORLD, YOU'RE BEATING ME, CRUEL WORLD
I'M BRUISED AND BROKEN BUT ALIVE.

GILBERT.

A MOTHER THAT DOESN'T TRUST YOU IS THE WORST.
I SAW THE SADDEST PICTURE ONCE
WHERE SANDRA DEE WAS SNOWBOUND IN A SHACK
WITH THIS YOUNG MOUNTAIN-CLIMBER
AND WHEN SHE GOT DOWN SAFELY THE NEXT MORNING
HER MOTHER WAS *SUSPICIOUS!*

VAL.

DID SHE DO ANYTHING WRONG?

GILBERT.

WELL HE DID TAKE HER IN HIS ARMS
BUT WHEN SHE STARTED TO RESPOND
THE CAMERA FADED TO A PICTURE
OF TWO BULLFROGS IN A POND
AND IT WAS LEFT UP TO THE AUDIENCE
WHO STILL DON'T KNOW TODAY
DID SANDRA DEE GO ALL THE WAY?

BOTH.

I'M BLUE TOO, SANDRA DEE
SANDRA DEE, SANDRA DEE
I'M LIKE YOU, SANDRA DEE
IF YOU EVER NEED A FRIEND
YOU CAN DEPEND ON ME
COUNT ON ME.

GILBERT.

THEY JUST LAID THERE BY THE FIRE
SLOWLY PUFFIN' ON A CIGGIE
WHILE THE CAMERA TOOK A SHOT
OF HOW THEIR TOES WERE PLAYIN' PIGGY
AND THEY GOT SO AWFUL DREAMY

FOR A MOMENT THERE IN FAC'
THAT I KEPT THINKIN' THEY WERE
GONNA HAVE TO BRING THE BULLFROGS BACK.

VAL.
A GIRL CAN GET A REPUTATION
OVER NUTHIN' AND I MEAN IT.
IF SHE EVEN DID THE SLIGHTEST
YOU WERE THERE AND WOULDN'VE SEEN IT.

GILBERT.
WELL, THEY REALLY KEPT YOU GUESSING
BUT I LIKED IT JUST THE SAME
'CAUSE SHE LOOKED SO AWFUL HAPPY
THE DAY THE BABY CAME.

BOTH.
I'M BLUE TOO, SANDRA DEE
SANDRA DEE, SANDRA DEE.
I'M LIKE YOU, SANDRA DEE
IF YOU EVER NEED A FRIEND
YOU CAN DEPEND ON
COUNT ON ME—SANDRA DEE, SANDRA DEE.

VAL. (*With a sigh, puts apple in pocket.*) Well—I guess that's all. (*Bows. Takes guitar.*) Farewell, O Princess Silver Bells! (*Goes Up Center.*)

(*MUSIC underscoring.*)

GILBERT. Oh, no! We can't, Val!

VAL. She's really knocked it all to pieces.

(*Chinese chatter from* GILBERT, *who bows, then goes Up Center to* VAL.)

GILBERT. Please, O, Princess Cherry Blossom, O, Shining Concubine of the East!

VAL. But what can we do?

GILBERT. But if we proved to her we didn't do anything—

VAL. (*Goes Right to below bench.*) How are we going to do that if she won't even listen?

GILBERT. (*An inspiration.*) She will to him!

VAL. You crazy or something?

GILBERT. I mean if we went to him ourselves, a personal appearance, and explained the whole situation and that your mother's real ape and ought to be locked up, I'll bet you he'd call her and tell her we hadn't done anything!

VAL. You mean talk to him face to face?

GILBERT. We've got to!

VAL. (*Going Right.*) Eeeeeeek!

GILBERT. (*Follows.*) You've got to, Val, it's our last fatal chance.

VAL. I couldn't. I just couldn't.

GILBERT. (*Happening to look Off.*) Quick! Someone's coming! Get in my locker!

(VAL *runs to* GILBERT'S *locker and jumps in.* GILBERT *slams the door and turns the lock.*)

VAL. (*After a moment.*) Who was it?

GILBERT. Nobody.

VAL. What are you doing?

GILBERT. I locked it. (*Puts locker key in her shoe.*)

(*MUSIC underscoring.*)

VAL. You can't.

GILBERT. I'll let you out after the last class. Then we'll go to his place together and we'll explain the whole thing!

GILBERT.

AND IN TIME YOU WILL SEE
IF YOU EVER NEED A FRIEND

VAL. Please, Gil, let me out! It's awful in here! Gil! . . . Gil! . . . Gil! . . .

YOU CAN DEPEND ON
COUNT ON ME—
SANDRA DEE, SANDRA DEE.

(GILBERT *dashes off Left to her class and* VAL *rides off Right yelling inside the locker.*)

BLACKOUT

ACT TWO

SCENE 6

Cocktail Bar. As furtive and shady-looking as ever, ORIENT *is at a remote table watching the Upstage entrance. If the lady should be accompanied by her husband, he is prepared to nip out through the kitchen. Befitting the occasion, a first meeting with one who sounded like a lady of quality, he has attired himself in a style that might be described as Madison Avenue Bohemian, even larger, darker glasses than usual. When* MRS.

BOYD *enters alone, smart and beautiful, he draws a deep sigh of relief and stands as the* WAITER *leads her to his table.*

MRS. BOYD. Mr. Orient?

ORIENT. (*Staring.*) This is almost beyond belief! First that voice—and now—you!

MRS. BOYD. I'm sorry—

ORIENT. Forgive me, dear lady. (*He kisses her hand.*) But somewhere—at some time—yours is a face that could never be forgotten. May I offer you—

(*The* WAITER *takes the cape from her shoulders.*)

MRS. BOYD. Nothing, thank you.

ORIENT. A coop de cafe peut-etre?

MRS. BOYD. (*Sits.*) I'm far too heartsick—

ORIENT. (*To the* WAITER.) Nothing, merci beaucaire. (*The* WAITER *exits Right.* ORIENT *sits next to* MRS. BOYD.) Tell me about it, will you?

MRS. BOYD. What really hurts—

ORIENT. I want you to tell me the whole story.

MRS. BOYD. What really stabs me to the heart—

ORIENT. Don't move! I have it! Renoir's Girl in April—in the Frick.

MRS. BOYD. Pardon!

ORIENT. The Frick Collection.

MRS. BOYD. Oh.

ORIENT. You are her, dear lady! Yours is that special face—but do go on, will you?

MRS. BOYD. As a mother—

ORIENT. Tell me. Were you ever on the stage?

MRS. BOYD. (*Modestly.*) Well—not really—

ORIENT. (*Reproachfully.*) And you with that voice of molten gold?

MRS. BOYD. I'm afraid it's a bit too late for me.

ORIENT. Was it too late for Princess Lee Radziwill? But do go on.

MRS. BOYD. But perhaps we gave Valerie too much tender loving care. We were so devoted to Dr. Spock, you know, until he branched out.

ORIENT. It's music! I swear it!

MRS. BOYD. (*Puzzled.*) Music?

ORIENT. Sitting here so close beside you, I can literally feel the vibrations of another artist! Do you play?

MRS. BOYD. Well—

ORIENT. I knew it! I knew the soul was there!

MRS. BOYD. I mean—when I think of that poor child out there all night in only a light mink—

ORIENT. That was the artist in you. We're really too sensitive, dear lady, all of us! We die ten thousand deaths every day—and yet—think of those heights of ecstasy we alone can know!

MRS. BOYD. Yes, there have been moments—

ORIENT. The artist embracing life with but one question: Do you or don't you?

MRS. BOYD. (*Startled.*) Do I what?

ORIENT. Live, dear lady! Live life to the hilt!

MRS. BOYD. I see.

(*MUSIC underscoring.*)

ORIENT. Oh, but we're the blessed of the gods, my dear, we artists! (*Sings.*)
TO BE ARTISTIC
IS STRANGE AND MYSTIC
LIKE YOUR SOUL WAS MADE
OF FLOWERS AND OF GRASS.

MRS. BOYD.
LET'S BE REALISTIC
TO BE ARTISTIC
IS TO FLOAT ABOVE
THE VULGAR AND THE CRASS.

ORIENT.
JOHN ADAMS PHRASED IT THUSLY
—"MAY OUR SONS BE STATESMEN
AND THEIR SONS
WITH BOTH HAND AND HEART
GIVE THEMSELVES TO ART."

MRS. BOYD.
YOU WOULD THINK THAT RONALD REAGAN HAD
SAID THAT.

ORIENT.
TO BE ARTISTIC
TO BE ARTISTIC
I'M NOT SURE IF WE'RE BLESSED
OR THE CURSED.
THE GREATLY GIFTED ARE FINELY SIFTED
BUT WITH PASSIONS WE MUST EXORCISE OR
BURST.
MEN KISS MEN WHEN THEY'RE ARTISTIC
IN ADMIRATION FOR A FELLOW MAN,
BUT COULD YOU GUESS
WHAT A BLOODY MESS
IF A GREEN BAY PACKER KISSED A RAM?

MRS. BOYD.
TO BE ARTISTIC
AND IDEALISTIC
YOU WOULD THINK WOULD MAKE ONE
HUMBLE AND BENIGN
BUT I'VE A COUSIN
WHO KNOWS A FELLOW
WHO HAD ACTUALLY HAD TEA
WITH GERTRUDE STEIN.
SHE MADE NO PROFOUND PRONOUNCEMENTS
AND WAS QUITE SARCASTIC TO THE CHAP
SO HE SAT BEREFT
AND BEFORE HE LEFT
HER POODLE PIDDLED ON HIS LAP.

BOTH.
LET'S BE REALISTIC
TO BE ARTISTIC
IS A SPARK OF HEAVEN
IN THE HUMAN BREAST.

ORIENT.
I KNOW FOR CERTAIN
THAT YOU'RE ARTISTIC
I'M AMAZED THAT UP TILL NOW
IT'S BEEN REPRESSED.

MRS. BOYD.
WELL, I DID ONCE WRITE A POEM—

ORIENT.
OH?

MRS. BOYD.
AND RECALL IT YET SOMEHOW

ORIENT. (*Lust.*) Recite your poem for me!

MRS. BOYD. Now?

ORIENT. Now!

MRS. BOYD. (*Recites.*)

I raced across a star-lit beach
My robes about me strewn.
And then exhausted on the sand
Was ravished by the moon.

ORIENT. Oh, magnificent!

BLACKOUT

ACT TWO

Scene 7

Exterior Orient's Apartment. The APARTMENT moves to its Upstage position, as People *walk down the street, an evening crowd. The street LIGHTS are on, and there is a dim GLOW from the apartment. After a moment,* Val *and* Gilbert *run Onstage.*

Gilbert. (*Runs to steps.*) This is it, come on! (*She starts up the steps.*)

Val. (*Fierce whisper, Up Left.*) Wait a minute! (Gilbert *goes back to* Val.) What if he isn't there?

Gilbert. (*Goes Center.*) He's there. Look, his lights are on. Someday you'll look back at this and thank me. Now come on.

Val. (*Breaks Down Left.*) Wait a minute!

Gilbert. What's the matter now? (*Crossing to her.*)

Val. What are you going to say to him?

Gilbert. Well—first I'll introduce us—Miss Valerie Boyd and Miss Marian Gilbert—and then we'll wait for him to invite us in.

Val. But what if he doesn't?

Gilbert. Then I'll request a few minutes of his time on a matter of great importance.

Val. What'll we do if he offers us a drink?

Gilbert. We'll just have to ask him what he's got.

Val. No whisky, you know!

Gilbert. Oh, no, nothing spiritual. (*Starting up again.*) Come on.

Val. (*Pulling away Down Left.*) But what else?

Gilbert. What do you mean, what else?

Val. We can't just sit around there drinking without saying anything.

Gilbert. (*Crossing to her.*) But how can I tell until the conversation starts flowing? But the main thing, we've got to tell him what a nut your mother is and then ask him if he'll be good enough to call her up and tell her we've never even said boo to him, much less anything else.

Val. You're not going to say anything about, you know, the way I feel about him, are you?

Gilbert. Of course not— (*Starts Right. Pulls* Val.) not unless the situation comes up.

Val. (*Stops* Gilbert.) Don't you dare, Marian Gilbert!

Gilbert. All right, if you don't want me to.

Val. You promise?

Gilbert. I promise. (*MUSIC.*) Now, come on.

VAL. (*Crosses Down Left.*) Of course, if the situation did come up . . .

GILBERT.
YOU LOOK LIKE A WOMAN IN LOVE WITH ME
FLUTTERING PULSE, MOISTURING BROW
HANDS THAT ARE CLAMMY AND TREMBLING.

VAL. Wow! (*Sings.*)
HENRY, SWEET HENRY.

(VAL *and* GILBERT *go to the steps of the brownstone,* GILBERT *first,* VAL *following. As* GILBERT *starts to push open the door, we hear:*)

MRS. BOYD. (*Inside house.*)
HENRY, SWEET HENRY.

GILBERT. (*To* VAL.) Somebody's coming!

MRS. BOYD. (*Off.*)
THESE HOURS WERE HEAVEN, HENRY—

GILBERT. Come on, Val. (*She runs down the steps and hides under the Orient apartment bay window.*)

MRS. BOYD. (*Off.*)
I SHALL PRIZE THEM ALWAYS—

(VAL *runs down the steps and hides Downstage of* GILBERT. *The outer door opens and* ORIENT'S *head peers out, glancing furtively up and down the street to see if the coast is clear. The* GIRLS *are out of his sight. Having scouted the street,* ORIENT *turns back and draws* MRS. BOYD *out of the shadows.*)

ORIENT. I have drunk deep of joy tonight, my darling, and now there can never be another wine in life for me.

MRS. BOYD. (*Smiles.*) What about tomorrow?

ORIENT. Tomorrow and tomorrow—and tomorrow. A quelle heure?

MRS. BOYD. A cinq heures peutetre?

ORIENT. Tres bon—carissima.

MRS. BOYD. Goodnight, sweet.

(*She goes off down the street, Off Right.* ORIENT *closes the door as he goes inside. The Stage is silent and empty for a long moment.* GILBERT *slowly emerges from under the bay window and looks at* VAL.)

GILBERT. Val? Val? (*No answer.*) Come on, Val. I'll never tell anybody, honest— (*Suddenly* VAL, *choking back a terrible sob, rushes from under the window and down the street in a different direction from the one her mother has taken.*) Val! Val! (*She starts to go after her, but something stops her. In such a moment of horror nobody wants to see anybody else. For another moment, she doesn't know what to do herself. Then she sits on the steps and covers her face in her arms and starts to cry for her friend.*)

BLACKOUT

ACT TWO

SCENE 8

Boyd Living Room. Night. The room is dim as VAL *enters wearily. As she starts to her room,* MR. BOYD, *who has been sitting in the chair, turns on a LAMP.*

MR. BOYD. Are you all right?

VAL. (*Few steps Right to above sofa.*) Yes, sir.

MR. BOYD. You've caused us a hell of a lot of worry, you know.

VAL. I'm sorry.

MR. BOYD. And Mrs. Gilbert too. I went to her house and talked to her after dinner. She was so upset I was going to call a doctor when Gil finally walked in.

VAL. (*Few steps back to Center.*) Did Gil say anything about where we were?

(MRS. BOYD *appears from her room tying the belt of her dressing gown and pauses to hear the answer to this question.* VAL'S *back is to her.*)

MR. BOYD. No—what was it— Mr. Orient again?

VAL. No, sir . . . That's all over.

MRS. BOYD. I should certainly hope so. Where were you?

VAL. (*After a pause.*) Just—goofing around—looking at the store windows.

MRS. BOYD. For twenty-four hours you've been looking at store windows?

VAL. Yes.

MRS. BOYD. Do you seriously expect me to believe that?

MR. BOYD. (*Rises.*) I don't think we ought to go on with this tonight. It's quite late and we're all tired and a little edgy. (*To* VAL *as* MRS. BOYD *goes to the desk for the mail.*) Are you hungry? Would you like a sandwich or a glass of milk?

VAL. No, thank you.

MR. BOYD. Then go on to bed now.

(VAL *starts to exit.*)

MRS. BOYD. Just one thing— (VAL *stops.*) In case you and Miss Gilbert happen to be planning any further adventures— I had a little talk with your Mr. Orient this afternoon and if you ever go anywhere near him again I've asked him to call me.

VAL. (*Starts to exit.*) He won't have to.

MRS. BOYD. And also— (VAL *stops.*) this association with the Gilbert girl is over with—done and finished.

MR. BOYD. You really think that's necessary?

MRS. BOYD. Definitely. Even her mother agrees about that. (*Down to sofa with mail.*) She says they've been in constant trouble ever since they started running around together.

VAL. (*Few steps Left.*) That's not true.

MRS. BOYD. (*Goes to sofa.*) That'll be enough out of you.

MR. BOYD. (*Puzzled. Few steps Center.*) When did Mrs. Gilbert tell you all this?

MRS. BOYD. Tonight. Didn't you get my message?

MR. BOYD. No.

MRS. BOYD. (*Sits.*) Oh, for God's sake, I told the operator to be sure and tell you I'd gone to see Mrs. Gilbert. (VAL *looks at her* FATHER.) I wanted to see just what sort of person she was. (VAL *looks back to her* MOTHER.) It was quite a revelation.

MR. BOYD. How?

MRS. BOYD. She couldn't have been less concerned. I was really quite shocked.

(VAL, *after pause, looks at her* FATHER.)

MR. BOYD. She can go to bed now, can't she?

MRS. BOYD. (*Vaguely disturbed.*) Of course. Good night, dear.

MR. BOYD. Good night, darling.

VAL. Good night, sir. Good night, mother.

(*She goes out.* MRS. BOYD *puts down the mail and mixes herself a drink.*)

MR. BOYD. What kind of fellow is this Mr. Orient?

MRS. BOYD. Oh, he was quite amused by it all.

MR. BOYD. What were they doing? Just following him around?

MRS. BOYD. Apparently that's all.

MR. BOYD. I'll bet that's what they were up to tonight, as a matter of fact.

MRS. BOYD. What do you mean?

MR. BOYD. Following him.

MRS. BOYD. But—she said not, didn't she?

MR. BOYD. Not actually. "Just goofing around" is probably just teenage for: "None of your damn business, Father dear." (*At this possibility, she is unable either to move or speak for a moment. The TELEPHONE rings.)* If it's for me, I've gone to bed.

MRS. BOYD. *(Rises, crosses to the phone and answers it.)* Hello . . . Oh yes, Mrs. Gilbert. . . . *(He stops and reads the papers he is carrying.)* Yes. . . . She just came in. Did Marian get back? . . . I see. No . . . not yet. I really haven't had a chance to talk to him. Thank you. Good night. *(She hangs up. What's the use of going on? It's all in the fan anyway.)* That was very stupid of me. The truth is, I ran into some friends and we had a nightcap at Twenty-one.

MR. BOYD. *(He studies her for a moment without emotion.)* It really doesn't matter any more.

(He exits Left. After a moment of thought, she dials a number. As she does so, her part of the SET moves Offstage and ORIENT'S *bed comes from the Right. A PHONE is ringing. Sleepily he removes his sequined sleep mask and gropes for the Right phone.)*

ACT TWO

SCENE 9

Orient's Bedroom.

ORIENT. Hello? . . . Macushla! *(Snapping upright.)* Oh, my God! . . . Are you sure? How big is he? *(By now he has grabbed his bedside address book and is going through it frantically.)* All right now, let's not panic, darling. You're not alone in this, you know, we'll see it through together, side by side. And to tell you the truth, I'm glad it's at last out in the open, I want the world to know—because neither of us has anything to be ashamed of, darling. *(Having dialed another number on the Left phone, he manages to sing into both.)*

FOREVER—
MAY I SPEAK WITH INDIA AIRWAYS PLEASE?
FOREVER—
YES, I SHALL HOLD ON, MISS HOROWITZ—
TWO HEARTS NOW INTERLOCK—
ONE TICKET TO BANGKOK—
NO LOVE WAS EVER GREATER—
CAN I FLY NOW AND PAY LATER?

FOREVER
I AM THROBBING NOW

TO PRESS YOU NEAR
FOREVER—
WILL YOU SHOW A FIRST-RUN MOVIE, DEAR?

(*As he sings, his BED is pulled off Right and Val's BEDROOM comes on from the Left. She is on the bed but not asleep.*)

ACT TWO

SCENE 10

Val's Bedroom. VAL *is dressed in pajamas and is lying on her bed.* MR. BOYD *enters Right.*

MR. BOYD. May I come in?

VAL. Yes, sir. (*Turns her head away from him. He sits on the bed and puts his hand on her shoulder.*)

MR. BOYD. Life is a little rough at times for everybody, darling, but nobody has it easy all the way. You know I'm a bit older than your mother and sometimes it's not easy for a wife to accept the difference.

VAL. I suppose so.

MR. BOYD. But then we don't have to go and shoot ourselves, do we?

VAL. No, sir.

MR. BOYD. How would you like to have lunch with me tomorrow? Just the two of us.

VAL. (*Moves to a kneeling position.*) I'd like that very much.

MR. BOYD. Good. We can talk things over—school and all that—before I go.

VAL. Go?

MR. BOYD. I'm planning to fly to London late tomorrow.

VAL. Oh.

MR. BOYD. It's a nuisance, but something came up suddenly.

VAL. That's all right; I understand.

MR. BOYD. (*Rises and goes Right a few steps. MUSIC underscoring.*) It's reached a point where half the time I don't know whether I'm running my business or my business is running me.

VAL. (*Sings.*)

DO YOU EVER GO TO BOSTON
ANY MORE?
NO, I GUESS YOU DON'T, OR ELSE
YOU'D MENTION IT.

REMEMBER HOW YOU TOLD ME I'D GET
SUNBURNED,

BUT I DIDN'T LISTEN
AND I GOT SUNBURNED
WHEN YOU TOOK ME TO THE BEACH.
YOU KNOW THAT BEACH
IN THAT PLACE AROUND NEAR BOSTON.

BOY, DID YOU HOLLER AT ME.
BOY WERE YOU CRANKY.
BUT I WAS SUNBURNED
AND YOU COULDN'T SPANK ME.

YOU GO TO BERLIN A LOT
YOU GO TO LONDON A LOT
AND I'VE MEANT TO ASK YOU
IF YOU EVER GO TO BOSTON.

DO YOU EVER GO TO BOSTON
ANY MORE?
DO YOU EVER GO TO BOSTON?

(MR. BOYD *moves back to the bed to sit beside* VAL. *He puts his arm around her. MUSIC continues.*)

MR. BOYD. How old were you then?

VAL. Five.

MR. BOYD. We closed our Boston office three years ago, but there can be other Bostons, you know. We can find all kinds of nice places to have a home if you want it.

VAL. You mean a real home?

MR. BOYD. Well, I'm pretty sick of hotel rooms myself.

VAL. For just you and me?

MR. BOYD. That's the way it looks, doesn't it?

VAL. (*Up on her knees.*) Where could we have it?

MR. BOYD. Well, where would you like it?

VAL. Wherever you could be home the most.

MR. BOYD. That won't matter any more, because I'm getting pretty fed up with all this traveling too. We'll just pick out the place we like the best and that'll be it.

VAL. Oh, Dad, do you really mean it?

MR. BOYD. I really mean it, sweetheart. It's all settled. (*Rises.*) I've still got to fly to London late tomorrow. (*Turns back to her.*) Is there any reason why you can't go with me? I mean you ought to be able to take a few days off from your school to— (VAL *has leaped off the bed and has run into his arms, almost knocking him over.*) Holy Moses! (*Holds her in his arms.*) There, there, take it easy, darling, take it easy. (*Pause.*) Do you think we can make a go of it?

GILBERT. Forever and ever. (*Off Right.*) Hey, Val! (VAL *doesn't answer.*) Val. . . .

(*MUSIC out.*)

VAL. (*Breaks aways from her* FATHER.) What's she doing here?

(GILBERT *enters in her "formal," almost incoherent with excitement.*)

GILBERT. Oh, hello, Mr. Boyd.
MR. BOYD. Hello.
GILBERT. They're here, Val!
VAL. (*Stiffly, her back to* GILBERT.) Whom is here?
GILBERT. (*Going Left, Downstage of* MR. BOYD *to* VAL.) The Knickerbocker Grey boys for the happening.
VAL. (*Turns to* GILBERT.) You mean here here?
GILBERT. Right in there with Kafritz and just wait'll you see them in their dress uniforms—hoo-boy!
MR. BOYD. I'm afraid not tonight, Marian.
VAL. I don't think I want to go, anyway.
GILBERT. When you look at them up close, they're really cute!
MR. BOYD. You see, she's very tired—
GILBERT. Mine's name is Hal and he's already a first sergeant!
MR. BOYD. I'm sure that at some other time—
VAL. That's yours, but what's mine like?
GILBERT. (*Sings.*)
WELL, TO ME HE SEEMS LIKE
THE DASHING TYPE
'CAUSE HE SHAVES ALREADY
AND HE SMOKES A PIPE!
VAL.
WELL, A PIPE IS FRANTICALLY ROMANTIC!

(*MUSIC continues under.*)

MR. BOYD. I am now going up on the roof and throw myself off.
VAL. (*Running to him, Downstage of* GILBERT. *Throws her arms around her* FATHER.) Okay, Dad, good night! (*Turns back to* GILBERT.) What else?
GILBERT. You'd really like him. He says he only got one look at you, but just flipped!

(MR. BOYD *exits Right.*)

VAL. (*Sings.*)
ARE YOU SURE IT'S ME HE WAS LOOKIN' AT?

HE COULD SEE ME NOW AND WANNA FALL DOWN FLAT!

(*MUSIC continues.*)

GILBERT. He said "the girl who was writing those letters." He likes girls who write letters.

VAL. Eeeeeek! (VAL *runs to her vanity and opens a box on top, containing make-up, perfume, etc.*) Here!

GILBERT. (*Joins* VAL *at the vanity.*) Wow!

VAL. (*Reads from container with eye shadow.*) "Desert Lust. To make her eyes reflect ancient nights along the Nile—"

GILBERT. What's this "Illicit"?

VAL. (*Takes perfume bottle from* GILBERT.) "When the woman of fire meets the man of ice—"

GILBERT. "Intimate Sin makes your mouth a scarlet gash!" (*Applies lipstick, then runs Down Left.*) Look out, Knickerbockers.

VAL. Gee, you look great! (*She goes to the armoire, opens it and takes out a dress to show* GILBERT.) How's this?

GILBERT. Zen-zational!

VAL. And you know what? (*She goes to the bed.*) I think I'll wear the mink tonight! (*She grabs the mink and starts to run off Right with the dress and the coat as:*)

BLACKOUT

ACT TWO

SCENE 11

It is the ballroom of the Waldorf. There are decorations, balloons, and steps in the rear. A group of GIRLS *in evening dresses are standing in a SPOTLIGHT, Center.* KNICKERBOCKER GREYS, *in dress uniforms, are standing to the sides. One by one, a girl joins a boy and they dance into the shadows.* GILBERT *dances with* RUSS. VAL *enters Up Right, comes down the steps and looks around for her boy.*

VAL. (*Sings.*)
HERE I AM
HEY, SOMEBODY
HERE I AM, HERE I AM.

I DON'T KNOW YOU,
YOU DON'T KNOW ME,
BUT HERE I AM.

HEY, SOMEBODY
WHO I DON'T EVEN KNOW,
HEY, SOMEBODY
THOUGH YOU MUST NEED ME SO
PLEASE TRY NOT TO CRY, SOMEBODY!

(HAL *enters from Left and goes toward* VAL.)

MY SOMEBODY
HI, SOMEBODY
HERE I AM!

(*He extends his hand and she joins him. They begin to waltz, then* RUSS *and* GILBERT *dance and in the next moment* ALL BOYS *and* GIRLS *are dancing.*)

CURTAIN

SCENE CHANGES AND PROP LIST

LOCKERS

ACT ONE—*Scene 2*

GILBERT
KAFRITZ
VAL
TEACHER (Beck)
NEVA, TERRY, ILENE } by locker

Bus—1—off Right

Leaves: out

School: in
Locker—3—on from Right
Bench—1—on from Right

Locker—4—on from Left
Bench—2—on from Left

Off Left:
VAL—paper bag with:
Note book
Papers
Tennis balls
2 books
Tennis racket

Personal:
GILBERT—coin

School: out

Bench—1—off Right
Locker—3—off Right
Bench—2—off Left (unload fast —load park bench)
Locker—4—off Left

Park 1: in
Park 2: in
Sun: in
Bench—2—on from Left

CENTRAL PARK ZOO

ACT ONE—*Scene 3*

ORIENT
STELLA
GILBERT
VAL
WOMAN (Wallace)
FITCH
WINELINE
CESAR
SCHATZ
SARGANT

School: out

Bench—1—off Right

Locker—3—off Right
Bench—2—on from Left
Lockers 4—off Left

Park 2: in
Bench—2—on from Left
Park 1: in
Sun: in

Off Right:
Bicycles:
CESAR
SCHATZ

Dark glasses—STELLA

Coin—WALLACE

Off Left:
Cane and tin cup—VAL
Dark glasses—VAL

Cane and tin cup—GILBERT
Dark glasses—GILBERT

Sailboats—FITCH and WINELINE

Dark glasses—ORIENT
Cigarettes—ORIENT
Lighter—ORIENT

Park 1: out
Park 2: out
Sun: out
Bench 2—off Left
Bldgs 7—down to mark
Bldgs 8—down to mark

Gin—in
Val—in
Gilbert's bureau—3—on from Right
Gilbert's bed—1—on from Right
Val's bed and table—2—on from Left

SOUND:
Lion roar
Lion roar

TWO BEDROOMS

ACT ONE—*Scene 4*

GIL
VAL
MRS. GILBERT

Park 1: out
Park 2: out
Sun: out
Park bench—2—off Left

Gil-Val—in
Gil's bureau and
Gil's bed—1—on from Right
Val's bed and table—2—on from Left
Off Up Right:
Telephone
Off Up Left:
Telephone

On Stage:
On table Right of bed:
Look Magazine

Gil's bed and bureau—1—off Right

Gil
Val: out
Val's bed, table—2—off Left

Carnegie Hall: in

CONCERT

ACT ONE—*Scene 5*

ORIENT
VAL
GIL
MRS. GILBERT
USHER (Sargant)

Val: out
Val's bed, table—2—off Left
Carnegie Hall: in

Flashlight—USHER
Ms. of music—on piano

Carnegie Hall: out
Desk and vanity—2—on from Right
Bed, table and record players: 4—on from Left
Armoire—6—on from Left

Val's bedroom: in

VAL'S BEDROOM

ACT ONE—*Scene 6*

VAL
GIL
MRS. BOYD

Piano—1—off Right

Carnegie Hall: out

Bldgs 7—up to mark
Bldgs 8—up to mark

Desk and chair—2—on from Left
Bed, table and record players: 4—on from Left
Armoire—6—on from Left

Val's bedroom: in

On Stage:
Album—on bed
Compass—in desk
Cover on bed
Dresses in armoire
Shoes in armoire

Val bedroom: out

Armoire—6—off Left
Bed—4—off Left
Desk and chair: 2—off Right

Soda fountain — 1 — on from Right
Table and chairs—3—on from Right
Table and chairs—5—on from Right
Magazine rack—raked on from Right

Soda shop: in

Right phone book—pushed on in one
Left phone book—pushed on in one

PHONE BOOTHS

ACT ONE—*Scene 7*

Val bedroom: out

Armoire and chair—6—off Left
Bed—2 tables—4—off Left
Vanity—2—off Right

Right phone booth—pushed on in one
Left phone booth—pushed on in one

LUNCHEONETTE

ACT ONE—*Scene 8*

GIL
VAL
KAFRITZ
KENNY
RUSS
HAL
SODA JERK
SALTANSTALL
AUCHINCLOSS
WHITNEY
VANDERBILT
STUYVESANT

Right phone booth—pulled off
Left phone booth—pulled off

Soda fountain—1—from Left
Table and chairs—3—on from Right
Table and chairs—5—on from Right
Magazine rack—raked on from Right

Soda shop: in
Off Left:
Bag with:
Scrapbook
2 composition books
2 pencils
2 coolie hats
Magazine
Whistle
Stick for KENNY

Soda shop: out

Soda fountain — 1 — off Left (unload and return to Right)
Table and chairs—3—off Right
Table and chairs—5—off Right
Magazine rack—raked off Right
Bldgs 7 and 8—down to mark

Street signs: in

Phone booth—raked on from Right
2 white trash cans: 6—on from Left
Empty plate—2—on from Right

STREET TELEPHONES

ACT ONE—*Scene 9*

ORIENT
STELLA
GIL
VAL
KAFRITZ
SALTANSTALL
AUCHINCLOSS
RUSS
HALL

Soda shop: out

Soda fountain — 1 — off Left (unload and return Right)
Table and chairs—3—off Right
Table and chairs—5—off Right
Magazine rack—raked off Right
Bldgs 7 and 8—down to mark

Street signs: in

Phone booth—Right—raked on
Phone booth—Left—raked on

Street signs: out

Phone book—raked off Right
Phone book—raked off Left

No. 3 portal masking wing: out to mark
Bldg 7—up to mark

Henry's apartment: 9—down to exterior mark
Henry's apartment exterior wing: 3—on to mark from Right

Moon: in

HENRY'S APARTMENT

ACT ONE—*Scene 10*

VAL
GIL
KAFRITZ
ORIENT
STELLA
COP (Brentte)
COP—FITCH
KENNY

Street signs: out

Phone booth: raked off Left

No. 3 portal masking wing: out to mark

Bldg 7—up to mark

Henry's apartment: 9—down to exterior mark

Henry's apartment exterior wing: 3—on to mark from Right

Moon: in

Off Right:
Police whistle
Nets
Ropes
Sign

Off Left:
Barricades
Bible

On Stage:
5 locks
Liquor bottles
Glass

Fire escapes — off Right and Left
Henry's apartment—9—pivot and up
Bldg 8—up to mark
Bldg 7—down to mark

No. 3 portal masking wing: in

Living-room unit—6—on from Left
Sofa and coffee table—1—on from Right
Phone table and chair—2—on from Left

HOTEL LIVING ROOM

ACT TWO—*Scene 1*

MR. BOYD
MRS. BOYD
COP (Brentte)
VAL
GIL

Fire escapes—off Right and Left

Henry's apartment: 9 — pivot and up

Bldg 8—up to mark
Bldg 7—down to mark

No. 3 portal masking wing: in

Living-room unit—6—on from Left

Phone table and chair—2—on from Left

Sofa and coffee table—1—on from Right

Off Left:
Bible
Phone

WASHINGTON SQUARE

ACT TWO—*Scene 2*

VAL
HIPPIES

Sofa-coffee table—1—off Right
Table-chairs—2—off Left
Wall unit—6—off Left

Houses 7 and 8—up

Washington 1: in
Washington 2: in
Washington 3: in

Bench

Bench—4—on (set at top)

Litter basket—off

Bench—4—off Right

Washington 1: out
Washington 2: out
Washington 3: out

Bldgs 7—up to mark

No. 3 portal masking wing: out to mark

Bldg 8—down to mark

Henry's apartment—9—down and pivot
Mrs. Boyd's chair and table—2—on from Left

ORIENT'S APARTMENT

ACT TWO—*Scene 3*

ORIENT
MRS. BOYD
VALERIE

Bench—6—off Left
Bench—3—off Right

Washington 1: out
Washington 2: out
Washington 3: out

Bldgs 7—up to mark
Bldgs 8—down to mark

No. 3 portal masking wing: out to mark

Henry's apartment—9—down and pivot

Mrs. Boyd chair and table—2—on from Left

Off Right:
Towel

On Stage:
Coffee cup and saucers—Boyd table
Screwdriver

Henry's apartment—9—up

No. 3 portal masking wing: in

Bldgs 7—down to mark
Bldgs 8—up to mark

Living room—6—on from Left

BOYD LIVING ROOM

ACT TWO—*Scene 4*

MRS. BOYD
MR. BOYD

Henry's apartment—9—up

No. 3 portal masking wing: in

Bldgs 7—down to mark
Bldgs 8—up to mark

Living room: 6—on from Left

Off Left:
Bible—MR. BOYD

On Stage:
Address book

Living-room unit—6—off Left

Mrs. Boyd chair and phone: 2—off Left

School: in

Locker—3—on from Right (back side)
Locker—4—on from Left (back side)

SCHOOL—Exterior Interior

ACT TWO—*Scene 5*

KAFRITZ
VAL
GIL
TEACHER (Beck)
FIRST GIRL
SECOND GIRL
THIRD GIRL
GIRL (Cesar)

Living-room unit—6—off Left

Mrs. Boyd chair and phone—2—off Left

School: in

Locker—3—on from Right (back side)
Locker—4—on from Left (back side)

On Stage:
Guitar—Val's locker

Bag with Hershey bar—GIL
Books—KAFRITZ

Bench—1—off Right
Bench—2—off Left

Locker—3—off Right
Locker—4—off Left

School: out

Cocktail bar: in

Banquet—2—on from Left

COCKTAIL BAR

ACT TWO—*Scene 6*

ORIENT
STELLA
MAITRE DE

Bench—1—off Right
Bench—2—off Left

Locker—3—off Right
Locker—4—off Left

School: out

Cocktail: in

Banquet—2—on from Left

On Stage:
On table:
Dark glasses
Martini

Cocktail: out

Banquet—2—off

Bldgs 8—down to mark

Bldg 7—up to mark

No. 3 portal masking wing: out to mark

Henry's apartment: 9—down to exterior mark

ORIENT'S APARTMENT—Exterior

ACT TWO—*Scene 7*

GIL
VAL
ORIENT
MRS. BOYD

Cocktail: out

Banquet—2—off

Bldgs 8—down to mark

Bldgs 7—up to mark

No. 3 portal masking wing: out to mark
Henry's apartment—9—down to exterior mark
Henry's apartment: 9—up

Bldgs 7—down to mark
Bldgs 8—up to mark

No. 3 portal masking wing: in

Living-room unit—6—on from Left

Sofa and coffee table—1—on from Right

Phone table and chair—2—on from Left

BOYD LIVING ROOM

ACT TWO—*Scene 8*

MR. BOYD
VAL
MRS. BOYD

Henry's apartment: 9—up

Bldgs 7—down to mark
Bldgs 8—up to mark

No. 3 portal masking wing: in

Living-room unit: 6—on from Left

Sofa and coffee table: 1—on from Right

Phone table and chair: 2—on from Left

On Stage:
Mail—desk
Tray with coffee table
Glass, decanter, ice bucket
Ash tray—table
Company reports—down Left

ORIENT'S BEDROOM

ACT TWO—*Scene 9*

Phone table and chair—2—moves off Left

Sofa and coffee table — 1 — moves off Left

Living-room unit—6—moves off Left

Henry's bed—3—moves on from Right

On Stage:
Address book

VAL'S BEDROOM

ACT TWO—*Scene 10*

Henry's bed—3—moves off Right

Val's bedroom: in

Vanity and chair—1—on from Left
Bed and table—4—on from Left
Armoire—6—on from Left

On Stage:
Dress on hanger: armoire

Vanity table:
Box on top with perfume

Vanity and chair: 1—off Left
Bed and table: 4—off Left
Armoire: 6—off Left
Val bedroom: out

Party No. 1: in
Party No. 2: in
Party No. 3: in

GOOD NEWS

MUSICAL COMEDY

By LAURENCE SCHWAB *and* B. G. DeSYLVIA

***Lyrics by* B. G. DeSylvia *and* Lew Brown**

***Music by* Ray Henderson**

10 males, 5 females, Singers, Dancers, Musicians, and Extras

GOOD NEWS is sparked with the tunes of the roaring twenties, when pork-pie hats and coonskin coats cluttered the campus. In story and song are recaptured the nostalgic memories of the days when the bobby-socker was called "flapper" and when a college campus was crowded with jalop-pies instead of jeeps. The then current collegiate craze was the "Varsity Drag." Against this background of youthful gaiety unfolds the story of Tom Marlowe, college football hero and campus casanova. Tom has flunked his astronomy examination, and things look mighty dark for the team. But then Tom's sweetheart Patricia induces her demure cousin Connie to tutor him. Tom digs in in real earnestness. The upshot of all this is that not only does Tom fall in love with Connie, but the Professor turns out to be tender-hearted after all and passes Tom on the eve of the big game. Then the game itself—what a game! Suspense runs high. Tom finally gets in the game and takes the pigskin across the goal line for the wining touchdown.

(Royalty, $50.00.)

THE MERRY WIDOW

OPERETTA

***Book and Lyrics by* CHARLES GEORGE**

***Music by* FRANZ LEHAR**

6 men, 12 women, and a mixed singing and dancing chorus
(As many as desired)
One interior set and modern costumes

All the celebrated song numbers are retained. This is a new and modern story of the romance of a dashing and handsome young Prince of the kingdom of Altruria and a beautiful young American widow. The comedy is clever and wholesome. The operetta is not difficult to cast and stage. The music will show your best singers to their greatest advantage. Suitable for any group from advanced High Schools to Civic and Professional Societies.

Libretto and vocal score $3.00 (Royalty, $50-$25.)

An eleven piece orchestration (an all-new arrangement) available at a rental charge of $10.00 a performance for the use of same, plus deposit.